Automatic Text Simplification

Synthesis Lectures on Human Language Technologies

Editor
Graeme Hirst, *University of Toronto*

Synthesis Lectures on Human Language Technologies is edited by Graeme Hirst of the University of Toronto. The series consists of 50- to 150-page monographs on topics relating to natural language processing, computational linguistics, information retrieval, and spoken language understanding. Emphasis is on important new techniques, on new applications, and on topics that combine two or more HLT subfields.

Automatic Text Simplification
Horacio Saggion
2017

Neural Network Methods for Natual Language Processing
Yoav Goldberg
2017

Syntax-based Statistical Machine Translation
Philip Williams, Rico Sennrich, Matt Post, and Philipp Koehn
2016

Domain-Sensitive Temporal Tagging
Jannik Strötgen and Michael Gertz
2016

Linked Lexical Knowledge Bases: Foundations and Applications
Iryna Gurevych, Judith Eckle-Kohler, and Michael Matuschek
2016

Bayesian Analysis in Natural Language Processing
Shay Cohen
2016

Metaphor: A Computational Perspective
Tony Veale, Ekaterina Shutova, and Beata Beigman Klebanov
2016

Automatic Text Simplification

Synthesis Lectures on Human Language Technologies

Editor

Graeme Hirst, *University of Toronto*

Synthesis Lectures on Human Language Technologies is edited by Graeme Hirst of the University of Toronto. The series consists of 50- to 150-page monographs on topics relating to natural language processing, computational linguistics, information retrieval, and spoken language understanding. Emphasis is on important new techniques, on new applications, and on topics that combine two or more HLT subfields.

Automatic Text Simplification
Horacio Saggion
2017

Neural Network Methods for Natual Language Processing
Yoav Goldberg
2017

Syntax-based Statistical Machine Translation
Philip Williams, Rico Sennrich, Matt Post, and Philipp Koehn
2016

Domain-Sensitive Temporal Tagging
Jannik Strötgen and Michael Gertz
2016

Linked Lexical Knowledge Bases: Foundations and Applications
Iryna Gurevych, Judith Eckle-Kohler, and Michael Matuschek
2016

Bayesian Analysis in Natural Language Processing
Shay Cohen
2016

Metaphor: A Computational Perspective
Tony Veale, Ekaterina Shutova, and Beata Beigman Klebanov
2016

Grammatical Inference for Computational Linguistics
Jeffrey Heinz, Colin de la Higuera, and Menno van Zaanen
2015

Automatic Detection of Verbal Deception
Eileen Fitzpatrick, Joan Bachenko, and Tommaso Fornaciari
2015

Natural Language Processing for Social Media
Atefeh Farzindar and Diana Inkpen
2015

Semantic Similarity from Natural Language and Ontology Analysis
Sébastien Harispe, Sylvie Ranwez, Stefan Janaqi, and Jacky Montmain
2015

Learning to Rank for Information Retrieval and Natural Language Processing, Second Edition
Hang Li
2014

Ontology-Based Interpretation of Natural Language
Philipp Cimiano, Christina Unger, and John McCrae
2014

Automated Grammatical Error Detection for Language Learners, Second Edition
Claudia Leacock, Martin Chodorow, Michael Gamon, and Joel Tetreault
2014

Web Corpus Construction
Roland Schäfer and Felix Bildhauer
2013

Recognizing Textual Entailment: Models and Applications
Ido Dagan, Dan Roth, Mark Sammons, and Fabio Massimo Zanzotto
2013

Linguistic Fundamentals for Natural Language Processing: 100 Essentials from Morphology and Syntax
Emily M. Bender
2013

Semi-Supervised Learning and Domain Adaptation in Natural Language Processing
Anders Søgaard
2013

Automatic Text Simplification

Horacio Saggion

ISBN: 978-3-031-01038-5   paperback
ISBN: 978-3-031-02166-4   ebook

DOI 10.1007/978-3-031-02166-4

A Publication in the Springer series
SYNTHESIS LECTURES ON HUMAN LANGUAGE TECHNOLOGIES

Lecture #32
Series Editor: Graeme Hirst, *University of Toronto*
Series ISSN
Print 1947-4040   Electronic 1947-4059

Automatic Text Simplification

Horacio Saggion
Department of Information and Communication Technologies
Universitat Pompeu Fabra

.

SYNTHESIS LECTURES ON HUMAN LANGUAGE TECHNOLOGIES #32

ABSTRACT

Thanks to the availability of texts on the Web in recent years, increased knowledge and information have been made available to broader audiences. However, the way in which a text is written—its vocabulary, its syntax—can be difficult to read and understand for many people, especially those with poor literacy, cognitive or linguistic impairment, or those with limited knowledge of the language of the text. Texts containing uncommon words or long and complicated sentences can be difficult to read and understand by people as well as difficult to analyze by machines. Automatic text simplification is the process of transforming a text into another text which, ideally conveying the same message, will be easier to read and understand by a broader audience. The process usually involves the replacement of difficult or unknown phrases with simpler equivalents and the transformation of long and syntactically complex sentences into shorter and less complex ones. Automatic text simplification, a research topic which started 20 years ago, now has taken on a central role in natural language processing research not only because of the interesting challenges it possesses but also because of its social implications. This book presents past and current research in text simplification, exploring key issues including automatic readability assessment, lexical simplification, and syntactic simplification. It also provides a detailed account of machine learning techniques currently used in simplification, describes full systems designed for specific languages and target audiences, and offers available resources for research and development together with text simplification evaluation techniques.

KEYWORDS

syntactic simplification, lexical simplification, readability measures, text simplification systems, text simplification evaluation, text simplification resources

To Sandra, Jonas, Noah, and Isabella

Contents

Acknowledgments

I am indebted to my fellow colleagues Stefan, Sanja, Biljana, Susana, Luz, Daniel, Simon, and Montserrat for sharing their knowledge and expertise with me.

Horacio Saggion
January 2017

CHAPTER 1

Introduction

Automatic text simplification is a research field in computational linguistics that studies methods and techniques to simplify textual content. Text simplification methods should facilitate or at least speed up the adaptation of available and future textual material, making accessible information *for all* a reality. Usually (but not necessarily), adapted texts would have information loss and a simplistic style, which is not necessarily a bad thing if the message of the text, which was in the beginning complicated, can in the end be understood by the target reader. Text simplification has also been suggested as a potential pre-processing step for making texts easier to handle by generic text processors such as parsers, or to be used in specific information access tasks such as information extraction. Simplifying for people is more challenging than the second use of simplification because the output of the automatic system could be perceived as inadequate in the presence of the least error.

The interest in automatic text simplification has grown in recent years and in spite of the many approaches and techniques proposed, automatic text simplification is, as of today, far from perfect. The growing interest in text simplification is evidenced by the number of languages which are targeted by researchers worldwide. Simplification systems and simplification studies exist at least for English [Carroll et al., 1998, Chandrasekar et al., 1996, Siddharthan, 2002], Brazilian Portuguese [Aluísio and Gasperin, 2010], Japanese [Inui et al., 2003], French [Seretan, 2012], Italian [Barlacchi and Tonelli, 2013, Dell'Orletta et al., 2011], Basque [Aranzabe et al., 2012], and Spanish [Saggion et al.].

1.1 TEXT SIMPLIFICATION TASKS

Although there are many text characteristics which can be modified in order to make a text more readable or understandable, including the way in which the text is presented, automatic text simplification has usually concentrated on two different tasks—lexical simplification and syntactic simplification—each addressing different sub-problems.

Lexical simplification will attempt to either modify the vocabulary of the text by choosing words which are thought to be more appropriate for the reader (i.e., transforming the sentence "The book was magnificent" into "The book was excellent") or to include appropriate definitions (e.g., transforming the sentence "The boy had tuberculosis." into "The boy had tuberculosis, a disease of the lungs."). Changing words in context is not an easy task because it is almost certain that the original meaning will be confused.

Syntactic simplification will try to identify syntactic phenomena in sentences which may hinder readability and comprehension in an effort to possibly transform the sentence into more readable or understandable equivalents. For example, relative or subordinate clauses or passive constructions, which may be very difficult to read by certain readers, could be transformed into simpler sentences or into active form. For example, the sentence "The festival was held in New Orleans, which was recovering from Hurricane Katrina" could be transformed without altering the original too much into "The festival was held in New Orleans. New Orleans was recovering from Hurricane Katrina."

As we shall later see, automatic text simplification is related to other natural language processing tasks such as text summarization and machine translation. The objective of text summarization is to reduce a text to its essential content which might be useful in simplification on occasions where the text to simplify has too many unnecessary details. The objective of machine translation is to translate a text into a semantic equivalent in another language. A number of recent automatic text simplification approaches cast text simplification as statistical machine translation; however, this approach to simplification is currently limited by the scarcity of parallel simplification data.

There is an important point to mention here: although lexical and syntactic simplification usually have been addressed separately, they are naturally related. If during syntactic simplification a particular syntactic structure is chosen to replace a complex construction, it also might be necessary to apply transformations at the lexical level to keep the text grammatical. Furthermore, with a text being a coherent and cohesive unit, any change at a local level (words or sentences) certainly will affect in one way or another textual properties (at the local and global level): for example replacing a masculine noun with a feminine synonym during lexical simplification will certainly require some languages to repair local elements such as determiners and adjectives, as well as pronouns or definite expressions in following or preceding sentences. Pragmatic aspects of the text, such as the way in which the original text has been created to communicate a message to specific audiences, are generally ignored by current systems.

As we shall see in this book, most approaches treat text simplification as a sequence of transformations at the word or sentence level, disregarding the global textual content (previous and following text units), thereby affecting important properties such as cohesion and coherence.

1.2   HOW ARE TEXTS SIMPLIFIED?

Various studies have investigated ways in which a given text is transformed into an easier-to-read version. In order to understand what text transformations would be needed and what transformations could be implemented automatically, Petersen and Ostendorf [2007] performed an analysis of a corpus of original and abridged CNN news articles in English (114 pairs), distributed by the Literacyworks organization,[1] aimed at adult learners (i.e., native speakers of English with poor reading skills). They first aligned the original and abridged versions of the news articles looking

---

[1]http://literacynet.org/

for the occurrence of an original-version sentence corresponding to a sentence in the abridged version. After having aligned the corpus, they observed that sentences from the original documents can be dropped (around 30%) or aligned to one (47% of same sentences) or more sentences (19%) in the abridged version (splits). The one-to-one alignments correspond to cases where the original sentence is kept practically untouched, cases where only part of the original sentence is kept, and cases of major re-writing operations. A small fraction of pairs of the original sentences were also aligned to a single abridged sentence, accounting for merges. Petersen and Ostendorf's study also tries to automatically identify sentences in the original document which should be split since those would be good candidates for simplification. Their approach consists of training a decision-tree learning algorithm (C4.5 [Quinlan, 1993]) to classify a sentence into split or non-split. They used various features including sentence length and several statistics on POS tags and syntactic constructions. Cross-validation evaluation experiments show that it is difficult to differentiate between the two classes; moreover, sentence length is the most informative feature, which explains much of the classification performance. Another interesting contribution is the study of dropped sentences, for which they train a classifier with some features borrowed from summarization research; however, the classifier is only slightly better than a majority baseline (i.e., not drop).

In a similar way, Bott and Saggion [2011b] and Drndarević and Saggion [2012a,b] identified a series of transformations that trained editors apply to produce simplified versions of documents. Their case in notably different from Petersen and Ostendorf [2007] given the characteristics of the language—Spanish—and target population of the simplified text version: people with cognitive disabilities. Bott and Saggion [2011b] analyzed a sample of sentence-aligned original and simplified documents to identify expected simplification operations such as sentence split, sentence deletion, and various types of change operations (syntactic, lexical, etc.). Moreover, additional operations such as insertion and reordering were also documented. Drndarević and Saggion [2012a,b] specifically concentrate on identifying lexical changes, in addition to synonym substitution, cases of numerical expression re-writing (e.g., rounding), named entity reformulation, and insertion of simple definitions. Like Petersen and Ostendorf [2007], Drndarević and Saggion train a Support Vector Machine (SVM) algorithm [Joachims, 1998] to identify sentences which could be deleted, improving over a robust baseline that always deletes the last sentence of the document.

1.3   THE NEED FOR TEXT SIMPLIFICATION

The creation of text simplification tools without considering a particular target population could be justifiable in that aspects of text complexity affect a large range of users with reading difficulties. For example, long and syntactically complex sentences are generally hard to process. Some particular sentence constructions, such as syntactic constructions which do not follow the canonical subject-verb-object (e.g., passive constructions), may be an obstacle for people with aphasia [Devlin and Unthank, 2006] or an autism spectrum disorder (ASD) [Yaneva et al., 2016b]. The same is true for very difficult or specialized vocabulary and infrequent words which can also prove difficult to understand for people with aphasia [Carroll et al., 1998, Devlin and Unthank, 2006] and ASD [Norbury, 2005]. Moreover, there are also certain aspects of language that prove difficult to specific groups of readers. Language learners, for example, may have a good capacity to infer information, although they may have a very restricted lexicon and may not be able to understand certain grammatical constructions. Dyslexic readers, in turn, do not have a problem with language understanding *per se*, but with the understanding of the written representation of language. In addition, readers with dyslexia were found to read better when using more frequent and shorter words [Rello et al., 2013b]. Finally, people with intellectual disabilities may have problems processing and retaining large amounts of information [Fajardo et al., 2014, Feng et al., 2009].

In order to create adapted versions for specific populations, various initiatives exist which promote accessible texts. An early proposal is Basic English, a language of reduced vocabulary of just over 800 word forms and a restricted number of grammatical rules. It was conceived after World War II as a tool for international communication or a kind of interlingua [Ogden, 1937]. Other initiatives are Plain English (see "Language for Special Purposes" in Crystal [1987]), for English in the U.S. and U.K., and the Rational French, a French-controlled language to make technical documentation more accessible in the context of the aerospace industry [Barthe et al., 1999]. In Europe, there are associations dedicated to the adaptation of text materials (books, leaflets, laws, official documents, etc.) for people with disabilities or low literacy levels, examples of which are the Easy-to-Read Network in Scandinavian countries, the Asociación Lectura Fácil[2] in Spain, and the Centrum för Lättläst in Sweden.[3] These associations usually provide guidance or recommendation about how to prepare or adapt textual material. Some such recommendations are as follows:

- use simple and direct language;

- use one idea per sentence;

- avoid jargon and technical terms;

- avoid abbreviations;

- structure text in a clear and coherent way;

- use one word per concept;

- use personalization; and

- use active voice.

---

[2]http://www.lecturafacil.net/
[3]http://www.lattlast.se/

These recommendations, although intuitive, are sometimes difficult to operationalize (for both humans and machines) and sometimes even impossible to follow, especially in the case of adapting an existing piece of text.

1.4   EASY-TO-READ MATERIAL ON THE WEB

Although adapted texts have been produced for many years, nowadays there is a plethora of simplified material on the Web. The Swedish "easy-to-read" newspaper *8 Sidor*[4] is published by the Centrum för Lättläst to allow people access to "easy news." Other examples of similarly oriented online newspapers and magazines are the Norwegian *Klar Tale*,[5] the Belgian *l'Essentiel*[6] and *Wablie*,[7] the Danish *Radio Ligetil*,[8] the Italian *Due Parole*,[9] and the Finnish *Selo-Uutiset*.[10] For Spanish, the Noticias Fácil website[11] provides easy-to-read news for people with disabilities. The Literacyworks website[12] offers CNN news stories in original and abridged (or simplified) formats, which can be used as learning resources for adults with poor reading skills. At the European level, the Inclusion Europe website[13] provides good examples of how full text simplifications and simplified summaries in various European languages can provide improved access to relevant information. The Simple English Wikipedia[14] provides encyclopedic content which is more accessible than plain Wikipedia articles because of the use of simple language and simple grammatical structures. There are also initiatives which aim to give access to easy-to-read material in particular and web accessibility in general the status of a legal right.

The number of websites containing manually simplified material pointed out above clearly indicates a need for simplified texts. However, manual simplification of written documents is very expensive and manual methods will be not cost-effective, especially if we consider that news is constantly being produced and therefore simplification would, in turn, need to keep the same pace. Nevertheless, there is a growing need for methods and techniques to make texts more accessible. For example, people with learning disabilities who need simplified text constitute 5% of the population. However, according to data from the Easy-to-Read Network,[15] if we consider people who cannot read documents with heavy information load or documents from authorities or governmental sources, the percentage of people in need of simplification jumps to 25% of

---

[4]http://8sidor.lattlast.se
[5]http://www.klartale.no
[6]http://www.journal-essentiel.be/
[7]http://www.wablieft.be
[8]http://www.dr.dk/Nyheder/Ligetil/Presse/Artikler/om.htm
[9]http://www.dueparole.it
[10]http://papunet.net/selko
[11]http://www.noticiasfacil.es
[12]http://www.literacyworks.org/learningresources/
[13]http://www.inclusion-europe.org
[14]http://simple.wikipedia.org
[15]http://www.easytoread-network.org/

the population.[16] In addition, the need for simplified texts is becoming more important as the incidence of disability increases as the population ages.

1.5   STRUCTURE OF THE BOOK

Having briefly introduced what automatic text simplification is and the need for such technology, the rest of the book will cover a number of relevant research methods in the field which have been the object of scientific inquiry for more than 20 years. Needless to say, many relevant works will not be addressed here; however, we have tried to cover most of the techniques which have been used, or are being used, at the time of writing. In Chapter 2, we will provide an overview of the topic of readability assessment given its current relevance in many approaches to automatic text simplification. In Chapter 3, we will address techniques which have been proposed to address the problem of replacing words and phrases by simpler equivalents: the lexical simplification problem. In Chapter 4, we will cover techniques which can be used to simplify the syntactic structure of sentences and phases, with special emphasis on rule-based linguistically motivated approaches. Then in Chapter 5, machine learning techiques, optimization, and other statistical techniques to "learn" simplification systems will be described. Chapters 6 and 7 cover very related topics—in Chapter 6 we will present fully fledged text simplification systems which have as users specific target populations, while in Chapter 7, we will cover sub-systems or methods specifically based on targeted tasks or user characteristics. In Chapter 8, we will cover two important topics: the available datasets for experimentation in text simplification and the current text simplification evaluation techniques. Finally, in Chapter 9, we close with an overview of the field and critical view of the current state of the art.

---

[16]Bror Tronbacke, personal communication, December 2010.

CHAPTER 2

Readability and Text Simplification

A key question in text simplification research is the identification of the complexity of a given text so that a decision can be made on whether or not to simplify it. Identifying the complexity of a text or sentence can help assess whether the output produced by a text simplification system matches the reading ability of the target reader. It can also be used to compare different systems in terms of complexity or simplicity of the produced output. There are a number of very complete surveys on the relevant topic of text readability which can be understood as "what makes some texts easier to read than others" [Benjamin, 2012, Collins-Thompson, 2014, DuBay, 2004]. Text readability, which has been investigated for a long time in academic circles, is very close to the "to simplify or not to simplify" question in automatic text simplification. Text readability research has often attempted to devise mechanical methods to assess the reading difficulty of a text so that it can be objectively measured. Classical mechanical text readability formulas combine a number of proxies to obtain a numerical score indicative of the difficulty of a text. These scores could be used to place the texts in an appropriate grade level or used to sort text by difficulty.

2.1 INTRODUCTION

Collins-Thompson [2014]—citing [Dale and Chall, 1948b]—defines text readability as the sum of all elements in textual material that affect a reader's understanding, reading speed, and level of interest in the material. The ability to quantify the readability of a text has long been a topic of research, but current technology and the availability of massive amounts of text in electronic form has changed research in computational readability assessment, considerably. Today's algorithms take advantage of advances in natural language processing, cognition, education, psycholinguistics, and linguistics ("all elements in textual material") to model a text in such a way that a machine learning algorithm can be trained to compute readability scores for texts. Traditional readability measures were based on semantic familiarity of words and the syntactic complexity of sentences. Proxies to measure such elements are, for example, the number of syllables of words or the average number of words per sentence. Most traditional approaches used averages over the set of basic elements (words or sentences) in the text, disregarding order and therefore discourse phenomena. The obvious limitations of early approaches were always clear: words with many syllables are not necessarily complex (e.g., children are probably able to read or understand complex dinosaur names or names of Star Wars characters before more-common words are acquired) and short sentences are not necessarily easy to understand (poetry verses for example). Also, traditional formulas were usually designed for texts that were well formatted (not web data) and relatively long. Most methods are usually dependent on the availability of graded corpora where documents are annotated with grade levels. The grades can be either categorical or ordinal, therefore giving rise to either classification or regression algorithmic approaches. When classification is applied, precision, recall, f-score, and accuracy can be used to measure classification performance and compare different approaches. When regression is applied, Root Mean Squared Error (RMSE) or a correlation coefficient can be used to evaluate the algorithmic performance. In the case of regression, assigning a grade of 4 to a 5th-grade text (1 point difference) is not as serious a mistake as it would be to assign a grade 7 to a 5th-grade text (2 points difference). Collins-Thompson [2014] presents an overview of groups of features which have been accounted for in the readability literature including:

- lexico-semantic (vocabulary) features: relative word frequencies, type/token ratio, probabilistic language model measures such as text probability, perplexity, etc., and word maturity measures;

- psycholinguistic features: word age-of-acquisition, word concreteness, polysemy, etc.;

- syntactic features (designed to model sentence processing time): sentence length, parse tree height, etc.;

- discourse features (designed to model text's cohesion and coherence): coreference chains, named entities, lexical tightness, etc.; and

- semantic and pragmatic features: use of idioms, cultural references, text type (opinion, satire, etc.), etc.

Collins-Thompson argues that in readability assessment it seems the model used—the features—is more important than the machine learning approach chosen. That is, a well-designed set of features can go a long way in readability assessment.

2.2   READABILITY FORMULAS

DuBay [2004] points out that over 200 readability formulas existed by the 1980s. Many of them have been empirically tested to assess their predictive power usually by correlating their outputs with grade levels associated with text sets.

Two of the most widely used readability formulas are the Flesch Reading Ease Score [Flesch, 1949] and the Flesch-Kincaid readability formula [Kincaid et al.]. The Flesch Reading Ease Score uses two text characteristics as proxies: the average sentence length *ASL* and the average number of syllables per word *ASW* which are combined in Formula (2.1):

$$Score = 206.835 - (1.015 * ASL) - (84.6 * ASW). \tag{2.1}$$

On a given text the score will produce a value between 1 and 100 where the higher the value the easier the text would be. Documents scoring 30 are very difficult to read while those scoring 70 should be easy to read.

The Flesch-Kincaid readability formula (2.2) simplifies the Flesch score to produce a "grade level" which is easily interpretable (i.e., a text with a grade level of eight according to the formula could be thought appropriate for an eighth grader).

$$GL = (0.4 * ASL) + (12 * ASW) - 15. \tag{2.2}$$

Additional formulas used include the FOG readability score [Gunning, 1952] and the SMOG readability score [McLaughlin, 1969]. They are computed using the following equations:

$$FOG = 0.4 * (ASL + HW) \tag{2.3}$$

$$SMOG = 3 + \sqrt{PSC}, \tag{2.4}$$

where HW is the percent of "hard" words in the document (a hard word is one with at least three syllables) and PSC is the polysyllable count—the number of words with 3 or more syllables in 30 sentences which shall be picked from the beginning, middle, and end of the document.

Work on readability assessment has also included the idea of using a vocabulary or word list which may contain words together with indications of age at which the particular words should be known [Dale and Chall, 1948a]. These lists are useful to verify whether a given text deviates from what should be known at a particular age or grade level, constituting a rudimentary form of readability language model.

Readability measures have begun to take center stage in assessing the output of text simplification systems; however, their direct applicability is not without controversy. First, a number of recent studies have considered classical readability formulas [Wubben et al., 2012, Zhu et al., 2010], applying them to sentences, while many studies on the design of readability formulas are based on considerable samples from the text to assess or need to consider long text pieces to yield good estimates; their applicability at the sentence level would need to be re-examined because empirical evidence is still needed to justify their use. Second, a number of studies suggest the use of readability formulas as a way to guide the simplification process (e.g., De Belder [2014], Woodsend and Lapata [2011]). However, the manipulation of texts to match a specific readability score may be problematic since chopping sentences or blindly replacing words could produce totally ungrammatical texts, thereby "cheating" the readability formulas (see, for example, Bruce et al. [1981], Davison et al. [1980]).

2.3   ADVANCED NATURAL LANGUAGE PROCESSING FOR READABILITY ASSESSMENT

Over the last decade, traditional readability assessment formulas have been criticized [Feng et al., 2009]. The advances brought forward in areas of natural language processing made possible a whole new set of studies in the area of readability. Current natural language processing studies in the area of readability assessment rely on automatic parsing, availability of psycholinguistic information, and language modeling techniques [Manning et al., 2008] to develop more robust methods. Today it is possible to extract rich syntactic and semantic features from text in order to analyze and understand how they interact to make the text more or less readable.

2.3.1   LANGUAGE MODELS

Various works have considered corpus-based statistical methods for readability assessment. Si and Callan [2001] cast text readability assessment as a text classification or categorization problem where the classes could be grades or text difficulty levels. Instead of considering just surface linguistic features, they argue, quite naturally, that the content of the document is a key factor contributing to its readability. After observing that some surface features such as syllable count were not useful predictors of grade level in the dataset adopted (syllabi of elementary and middle school science courses of various readability levels from the Web), they combined a unigram language model with a sentence-length language model in the following approach:

$$P_c(g|d) = \lambda * P_a(g|d) + (1 - \lambda) * P_b(g|d), \qquad (2.5)$$

where g is a grade level, d is the document, P_a is a unigram language model, P_b is a sentence-length distribution model, and λ is a coefficient adjusted to yield optimal performance. Note that probability parameters in P_a are words, that is the document should be seen as $d = w_1 \ldots w_n$ with w_l the word at position l in the document, while in probability P_b the parameters are sentence lengths, so a document with k sentences should be thought as $d = l_1 \ldots l_k$ with l_i the length of the i-th sentence. The P_a probability distribution is a unigram model computed in the usual way using Bayes's theorem as:

$$P_a(g|d) = \frac{P(d|g)P(g)}{P(d)}. \qquad (2.6)$$

The probabilities are estimates obtained by counting events over a corpus. Where P_b is concerned, a normal distribution model with specific mean and standard deviation is proposed. The combined model of content and sentence length achieves an accuracy of 75% on a blind test set, while the Flesch-Kincaid readability score will just predict 21% of the grades correctly.

2.3.2   READABILITY AS CLASSIFICATION

Schwarm and Ostendorf [2005] see readability assessment as classification and propose the use of SVM algorithms for predicting the readability level of a text based on a set of textual features. In order to train a readability model, they rely on several sources: (i) documents collected from the *Weekly Reader*[1] educational newspaper with 2nd–5th grade levels; (ii) documents from the *Encyclopedia Britannica* dataset compiled by Barzilay and Elhadad [2003] containing original

---

[1]http://www.weeklyreader.com

encyclopedic articles (115) and their corresponding children's versions (115); and (iii) CNN news stories (111) from the LiteracyNet[2] organization available in original and abridged (or simplified) versions. They borrow the idea of Si and Callan [2001], thus devising features based on statistical language modeling. More concretely, given a corpus of documents with say grade k, they create a language model for that grade. Taking 3-gram sequences as units for modeling the text, the probability $p(w)$ of a word sequence $w = w_1 \ldots w_n$ in the k-grade corpus is computed as:

$$p(w) = p(w_1)p(w_2|w_1) * \prod_{i=3}^{n} p(w_i|w_{i-1}, w_{i-2}). \tag{2.7}$$

where the 3-gram probabilities are estimated using 3-gram frequencies observed in the k-grade documents and smoothing techniques to account for unobserved events. Given the probabilities of a sequence w in the different models (one per grade), a likelihood ratio of sequence w is defined as:

$$LR(w, k) = \frac{p(w|k)p(k)}{\sum_{c \neq k} p(w|c)p(c)}, \tag{2.8}$$

where the prior $p(k)$ probabilities can be assumed to be uniform. The $LR(w, k)$ values already give some information on the likelihood of the text being of a certain complexity or grade. Additionally, the authors use perplexity as an indicator of the fit of a particular text to a given model where low perplexity for a text t and model m would indicate a better fit of t to m. Worth noting is the reduction of the features of the language models based on feature filtering by information gain (IG) values to 276 words (the most discriminative) and 56 part of speech tags (for words not selected by IG). SVMs are trained using the graded dataset (*Weekly Reader*), where each text is represented as a set of features including traditional readability assessment superficial features such as average sentence length, average number of syllables per word, and the Flesch-Kincaid index together with more-sophisticated features such as syntax-based features, vocabulary features, and language model features. Syntax-based features are extracted from parsed sentences [Charniak, 2000] and include average parse tree height, average number of noun phrases, average number of verb phrases, and average number of clauses (SBARs in the Penn Treebank tag set[3]). Vocabulary features account for out-of-vocabulary (OOV) word occurrences in the text. These are computed as percentages of words or word types not found in the most common 100, 200, and 500 words occurring in 2nd-grade texts. Concerning language model features, there are 12 perplexity values for 12 different language models computed using 12 different combinations of the paired datasets Britannica/CNN (adults vs. children) and three different n-grams: unigrams, bigrams, and trigrams (combining discriminative words and POS tags). The authors obtained better results in comparison to traditional readability formulas when their language model features are used in combination with vocabulary features, syntax-based features, and superficial indicators. Petersen and Ostendorf [2007] extend the previous work by considering additional non-graded

---

[2]http://literacynet.org/
[3]https://www.ling.upenn.edu/courses/Fall_2003/ling001/penn_treebank_pos.html

data from newspaper articles to represent higher grade levels (more useful for classification than for regression).

2.3.3   DISCOURSE, SEMANTICS, AND COHESION IN ASSESSING READABILITY

Feng et al. [2009] are specially interested in readability for individuals with mild-level intellectual disabilities (MID) (e.g., intelligence quotient (IQ) in the 55–70 range) and how to select appropriate reading material for this population. The authors note that people with MID are different from adults with low literacy in that the former have problems with working memory and with discourse representation, thereby complicating the processes of recalling information and inference as they read a text. The authors argue that appropriate readability assessment tools which take into account the specific issues of these users should therefore be designed. Their main research hypothesis being that the number of entity mentions in a text should be related to readability issues for people with MID, they design a series of features accounting for entity density. Where data for studying this specific population is concerned, they have created a small (20 documents in original and simplified versions) but rather unique ID dataset for testing their readability prediction model. The dataset is composed of news documents with aggregated readability scores based on the number of correct answers to multiple choice questions that 14 MID individuals had given after reading the texts. In order to train a model, they rely on the availability of paired and generic graded corpora. The paired dataset (not graded) is composed of original articles from *Encyclopedia Britannica* written for adults and their adapted versions for children and CNN news stories from the LiteracyNet organization available in original and abridged (or simplified) versions. The graded dataset is composed of articles for students in grades 2–5. Where the model's features are concerned, although many features studied were already available (or similar) in previous work, novel features take into account the number and the density of entity mentions (i.e., nouns and named entities), the number of lexical chains in the text, average lexical chain length, etc. These features are assessed on the paired datasets so as to identify their discriminative power, leaving all but two features outside the model. Three rich readability prediction models (corresponding to basic, cognitively motivated, and union of all features) are then trained on the graded dataset (80% of the dataset) using a linear regression algorithm (unlike the above approach). Evaluation is carried out on 20% of the dataset, showing considerable error reduction (difference between predicted and gold grade) of the models when compared with a baseline readability formula (the Flesch-Kincaid index [Kincaid et al.]). The final user-specific evaluation is conducted on the ID corpus where the model is evaluated by computing the correlation between system output and human readability scores associated with texts.

Feng et al. [2010] extended the previous work by incorporating additional features (e.g., language model features and out-of-vocabulary features from Schwarm and Ostendorf [2005] and entity coreference and coherence-based features based on those of Barzilay and Lapata [2008] and Pitler and Nenkova [2008]), assessing performance of each group of features, and comparing their model to state-of-the-art competing approaches (i.e., mainly replicating the models of Schwarm and Ostendorf [2005]). Experimental results using SVMs and logistic regression classifiers show that although accuracy is still limited (around 74% with SVMs and selected features) important gains are obtained from the use of more sophisticated linguistically motivated features.

Heilman et al. [2007] are interested in the effect of **pedagogically motivated features** in the development of readability assessment tools, especially in the case of texts for second language (L2) learners. More specifically, they suggest that since L2 learners acquire lexicon and grammar of the target language from exposure to material specifically chosen for the acquisition process, both lexicon and grammar should play a role in assessing the reading difficulty of the L2 learning material. In terms of lexicon, a unigram language model is proposed for each grade level so as to assess the likelihood of a given text to a given grade (see Section 2.3.1 for a similar approach). Where syntactic information is concerned, two different sets of features are proposed: (i) a set of 22 grammatical constructions (e.g., passive voice, relative clause) identified in sentences after being parsed by the Stanford Parser [Klein and Manning, 2003], which produces syntactic constituent structures; and (ii) 12 grammatical features (e.g., sentence length, verb tenses, part of speech tags) which can be identified without the need of a syntactic parser. All feature values are numerical, indicating the number of times the particular feature occurred per word in the text (note that other works take averages on a per-sentence basis). Texts represented as vectors of features and values are used in a k-Nearest Neighbor (kNN) algorithm (see Mitchell [1997]) to predict the readability grade of unseen texts: a given text t is compared (using a similarity measure) to all available vectors and the k-closest texts retrieved, the grade level of t is then the most frequent grade among the k retrieved texts. While the lexical model above will produce, for each text and grade, a probability, the confidence of the kNN prediction can be computed as the proportion of the k texts with same class as text t. The probability of the language model together with the kNN confidence can be interpolated yielding a confidence score to obtain a joint grade prediction model. In order to evaluate different individual models and combinations, the authors use one dataset for L1 learners (a web corpus [Collins-Thompson and Callan, 2004]) and a second dataset for L2 learners (collected from several sources). Prediction performance is carried out using correlation and MSE, since the authors argue regression is a more appropriate way to see readability assessment. Overall, although the lexical model in isolation is superior to the two grammatical models (in both datasets), their combination shows significant advantages. Moreover, although the complex syntactic features have better predictive power than the simple syntactic features, their slight difference in performance may justify not using a parser.

Although these works are interesting because they consider a different user population, they still lack an analysis of the effect that different automatic tools have in readability assessment performance: since parsers, coreference resolution systems, and lexical chainers are imperfect, an important question to be asked is how changes in performance affect the model outcome.

Crossley et al. [2007] investigate three Coh-Metrix variables [Graesser et al., 2004] for assessing the readability of texts from the Bormuth corpus, a dataset where scores are given to texts based on aggregated answers from informants using cloze tests. The number of words per sentence as an estimate of syntactic complexity, argument overlap—the number of sentences sharing an argument (noun, pronouns, noun phrases)—, and word frequencies from the CELEX database [Celex, 1993] were used in a multiple regression analysis. Correlation between the variables used and the text scores was very high.

Flor and Klebanov [2014] carried out one of the few studies (see Feng et al. [2009]) to assess lexical cohesion [Halliday and Hasan, 1976] for text readability assessment. Since cohesion is related to the way in which elements in the text are tied together to allow text understanding, a more cohesive text may well be perceived as more readable than a less cohesive text. Flor and Klebanov define lexical tightness, a metric based on a normalized form of pointwise mutual information by Church and Hanks [1990] (NPMI) that measures the strength of associations between words in a given document based on co-occurrence statistics compiled from a large corpus. The lexical tightness of a text is the average of NPMIs values of all content words in the text. It is shown that lexical tightness correlates well with grade levels: simple texts tend to be more lexically cohesive than difficult ones.

2.4   READABILITY ON THE WEB

There is increasing interest in assessing document readability in the context of web search engines and in particular for personalization of web search results: search results that, in addition to matching the user's query, are ranked according to their readability (e.g., from easier to more difficult). One approach is to display search results along with readability levels (Google Search offered in the past the possibility of filtering search results by reading level) so that users could select material based on its reading level assessment; however, this is limited in that the profile or expertise of the reader (i.e., search behavior) is not taken into consideration when presenting the results. Collins-Thompson et al. [2011] introduced a tripartite approach to personalization of search results by reading level (appropriate documents for the user's readability level should be ranked higher) which takes advantage of user profiles (to assess their readability level), document difficulty, and a re-ranking strategy so that documents more appropriate for the reader would move to the top of the search result list. They use a language-model readability assessment method which leverages word difficulty computed from a web corpus in which pages have been assigned grade levels by their authors [Collins-Thompson and Callan, 2004]. The method departs from traditional readability formulas in that it is based on a probabilistic estimation that models individual word complexity as a distribution across grade levels. Text readability is then based on distribution of those words occurring in the document. The authors argue that traditional formulas which consider morphological word complexity and sentence complexity (e.g., length) features and that sometimes require word-passages of certain sizes (i.e., at least 100 words) to yield an accurate readability estimate appear inappropriate in a web context where sentence boundaries are sometimes nonexistent and pages can have very little textual content (e.g., images and captions). To estimate the reading proficiency of users and also to train some of the model parameters and evaluate their approach, they rely on the availability of proprietary data on user-interaction behaviors with a web search engine (containing queries, search results, and relevance assessment). With this dataset at hand, the authors can compute a distribution of the probability that a reader likes the readability level of a given web page from web pages that the user visited and read. A re-ranking algorithm, LambdaMART [Wu et al., 2010], is then used to improve the search results and bring results more appropriate to the user to the top of the search result list. The algorithm is trained using reading level for pages and snippets (i.e., search results summaries), user reading level, query characteristics (e.g., length), reading level interactions (e.g., snippet-page, query-page), and confidence values for many of the computed features. Re-ranking experiments across a variety of query-types indicate that search results improve at least one rank for all queries (i.e., the appropriate URL was ranked higher than with the default search engine ranking algorithm). Related to work on web documents readability is the question of how different ways in which web pages are parsed (i.e., extracting the text of the document and identifying sentence boundaries) influence the outcome of traditional readability measures. Palotti et al. [2015] study different tools for extracting and sentence-splitting textual content from pages and different traditional readability formulas. They found that web search results ranking varies considerably depending on different readability formulas and text processing methods used and also that some text processing methods would produce document rankings with marginal correlation when a given formula is used.

2.5   ARE CLASSIC READABILITY FORMULAS CORRELATED?

Given the proliferation of readability formulas, one may wonder how they differ and which one should be used for assessing the difficulty of a given text. Štajner et al. [2012] study the correlation of a number of classic readability formulas and linguistically motivated features using different corpora to identify which formula or linguistic characteristics may be used to select appropriate text for people with an autism-spectrum disorder.

The corpora included in the study were: 170 texts from Simple Wikipedia, 171 texts from a collection of news texts from the METER corpus, 91 texts from the health section of the British National Corpus, and 120 fiction texts from the FLOB corpus.[4] The readability formulas studied were the Flesch Reading Ease score, the Flesch-Kincaid grade level, the SMOG grading, and FOG index. According to the authors, the linguistically motivated features were designed to detect possible "linguistic obstacles" that a text may have to hinder readability. They include features of structural complexity such as the average number of major POS tags per sentence, average number of infinitive markers, coordinating and subordinating conjunctions, and prepositions. Features indicative of ambiguity include the average number of sentences per word, average number of pronouns and definite descriptions per sentence. The authors first computed over each

---

[4]http://www.helsinki.fi/varieng/CoRD/corpora/FLOB/

corpus averages of each readability score to identify which corpora were "easier" according to the formulas. To their surprise and according to all four formulas, the corpus of fiction texts appears to be the easiest to read, with health-related documents at the same readability level as Simple Wikipedia articles. In another experiment, they study the correlation of each pair of formulas in each corpus; their results indicate almost perfect correlation, indicating the formulas could be interchangeable. Their last experiment, which studies the correlation between the Flesch-Kincaid formula and the different linguistically motivated features, indicates that although most features are strongly correlated with the readability formula, the strength of the correlation varies from corpus to corpus. The authors suggest that because of the correlation of the readability formula with linguistic indicators of reading difficulty, the Flesch score could be used to assess the difficulty level of texts for their target audience.

2.6   SENTENCE-LEVEL READABILITY ASSESSMENT

Most readability studies consider the text as the unit for assessment (although Collins-Thompson et al. [2011] present a study also for text snippets and search queries); however, some authors have recently become interested in assessing readability of short units such as sentences. Dell'Orletta et al. [2014a,b], in addition to presenting a readability study for Italian where they test the value of different features for classification of texts into easy or difficult, also address the problem of classifying sentences as easy-to-read or difficult-to-read. The problem they face is the unavailability of annotated corpora for the task, so they rely on documents from two different providers: easy-to-read documents are sampled from the easy-to-read newspaper *Due Parole*[5] while the difficult-to-read documents are sampled from the newspaper *La Repubblica*.[6] Features for document classification included in their study are: raw text features such as sentence-length and word-length averages, lexical features such as type/token ratio (i.e., lexical variety) and percentage of words on different Italian word reference lists, etc., morpho-syntactic features such as probability distributions of POS tags in the text, ratio of the number of content words (nouns, verbs, adjectives, adverbs) to number of words in the text, etc., and syntactic features such as average depth of syntactic parse trees, etc. For sentence readability classification (easy-to-read vs. difficult-to-read), they prepared four different datasets based on the document classification task. Sentences from *Due Parole* are considered easy-to-read; however, assuming that all sentences from *La Reppublica* are difficult would in principle be an incorrect assumption. Therefore, they create four different sentence classification datasets for training models and assess the need for manually annotated data: the first set (s1) is a balanced dataset of easy-to-read and difficult-to-read sentences (1310 sentences of each class); the second dataset (s2) is an un-balanced dataset of easy-to-read (3910 sentences) and assumed difficult-to-read sentences (8452), the third dataset (s3) is a balanced dataset with easy-to-read (3910 sentences) and assumed difficult-to-read sentences (3910); and, finally, the fourth dataset (s4) also contains easy-to-read sentences (1310) and assumed difficult-

---

[5]http://www.dueparole.it/default_.asp
[6]http://www.repubblica.it/

to-read sentences (1310). They perform classification experiments with maximum entropy models to discriminate between easy-to-read and difficult-to-read sentences, using held-out manually annotated data. They noted that although using the gold-standard dataset (s1) provides the best results in terms of accuracy, using a balanced dataset of "assumed" difficult-to-read sentences (i.e., s3) for training is close behind, suggesting that one should trade off the efforts of manually filtering out difficult-sentences to create a dataset. They additionally study feature contribution to sentence readability and document readability, noting that local features based on syntax are more relevant for sentence classification while global features such as average sentence and word lengths or token/type ratio are more important for document readability assessment.

Vajjala and Meurers [2014] investigate the issue of readability assessment for English, also focusing on the readability of sentences. Their approach is based on training two different regression algorithms on WeeBit, a corpus of 625 graded documents for age groups 7 to 16 years that they have specifically assembled, which contains articles from the Weekly Reader (see above) and articles from the BBCBitesize website. As in previous work, the model contains a number of different groups of features accounting for lexical and POS tag distribution information, superficial characteristics (e.g., word length) and classical readability indices (e.g., Flesch-Kincaid), age-of-acquisition word information, word ambiguity, etc., 10-fold cross-validation evaluation, using correlation and means error rate metrics, is carried out as is validation on available standard datasets from the Common Core Standards corpus[7] (168 documents), the TASA corpus (see Vajjala and Meurers [2014] for details) (37K documents), and the Math Readability corpus[8] (120 web pages). The model achieves high correlation in cross-validation and reasonable correlation across datasets, except in the Math corpus probably because of the rating scale used. The approach also compares very favorably with respect to several proprietary systems. Where sentence readability is concerned, the model trained on the WeeBit corpus is applied to sentences from the OneStopEnglish corpus,[9] a dataset in which original documents (30 articles, advanced level) have been edited to obtain documents at intermediate and beginner reading levels. Experiments are first undertaken to assess whether the model is able to separate the three different types of documents, and then to evaluate a sentence readability model. To evaluate sentence readability, each pair of parallel documents (advanced-intermediate, intermediate-beginner, advanced-beginner) is manually sentence-aligned and experiments are carried out to test whether the model is able to preserve the relative readability order of the aligned sentences (e.g., advanced-level sentence less readable than beginner-level sentence). Overall, the model preserves the readability order in 60% of the cases.

---

[7]http://www.corestandards.org/ELA-Literacy/
[8]http://wing.comp.nus.edu.sg/downloads/mwc/
[9]http://www.onestopenglish.com/

2.7   READABILITY AND AUTISM

Yaneva et al. [2016a,b] study text and Web accessibility for people with ASD. They developed a small corpus composed of 27 documents evaluated by 27 people diagnosed with an ASD. The novelty of the corpus is that, in addition to induced readability levels, it also contains gaze data obtained from eye-tracking experiments in which ASD subjects (and a control group of non-ASD subjects) were measured reading the texts, after which they were asked multiple-choice text-comprehension questions. The overall difficulty of the texts was obtained from quantitative data relating to answers given to those comprehension questions. Per each text, correct and incorrect answers were counted and text ranked based on number of correct answers. The ranking provided a way to separate texts into three difficulty levels: easy, medium, and difficult. The corpus itself was not used to develop a readability model; instead, it was used as test data for a readability model trained on the WeeBit corpus (see previous section), which was transformed into a 3-way labeled dataset (only 3 difficulty levels were extracted from WeeBit to comply with the ASD corpus).

Yaneva et al. grouped sets of features according to the different types of phenomena that account for: (i) lexico-semantic information such as word characteristics (length, syllables, etc.), numerical expressions, passive verbs, etc.; (ii) superficial syntactic information such as sentence length or punctuation information; (iii) cohesion information such as occurrence of pronouns and definite descriptions, etc.; (iv) cognitively motivated information including word frequency, age of acquisition of words, word imagability, etc.; and (v) information arising from several readability indices such as the Flesch-Kincaid Grade Level and the FOG readability index, etc. Two decision-tree algorithms, random forest [Breiman, 2001] and reduced error pruning tree (see [Hall et al., 2009]), were trained on the WeeBit corpus (see previous section) and cross-validated in WeeBit and tested in the ASD corpus. Feature optimization was carried out using a best-first feature selection strategy which identified such features as polysemy, FOG index, incidence of pronouns, sentence length, age of acquisition, etc. The feature selection procedure yields a model with improved performance on training and test data; nonetheless, results of the test on the ASD corpus are not optimal when compared with the cross-validation results on WeeBit. Worth noting is that although some of the features selected might be representative of problems ASD subjects may encounter when reading text, these features emerged from a corpus (WeeBit) that is not ASD-specific, suggesting that the selected features model general text difficulty assessment.

Based on the ASD corpus, a sentence readability assessment dataset was prepared composed of 257 sentences. Sentences were classified into easy-to-read and difficult based on the eye-tracker data associated with the texts. Sentences were ranked based on the average number of fixations they had during the readability assessment experiments and the set of sentences split in two parts to yield the two sentence readability classes. To complement the sentences from ASD and to control for length, short sentences from publicly available sources [Laufer and Nation, 1999] were added to the dataset. The labels for these sentences were obtained through a comprehension questionnaire which subjects with ASD had to answer. Sentences were considered easy to read if at least 60% of the subjects answered correctly the comprehension question associated with the sentence. Binary classification experiments on this dataset were performed using the Pegasos algorithm [Shalev-Shwartz et al., 2007] with features to model superficial sentence characteristics (number of words, word length, etc.), cohesion (proportion of connectives, causal expressions, etc.), cognitive indicators (word concreteness, imagability, polysemy, etc.), and several incidence counts (negation, pronouns, etc.). A cross-validation experiment achieved 0.82 F-score using a best-first feature selection strategy.

2.8   CONCLUSION

Over the years researchers have tried to come up with models able to predict the difficulty of a given text. Research on readability assessment is important for automatic text simplification in that models of readability assessment can help identify texts or text fragments which would need some sort of adaptation in order to made them accessible for a specific audience. Readability assessment can also help developers in the evaluation of automatic text simplification systems. Although traditional formulas which rely on simple superficial proxies are still used, in recent years, the availability of sophisticated natural language processing tools and better understanding of text properties accounting for text quality, cohesion, and coherence have fueled research in readability assessment, notably in computational linguistics.

This chapter covered several aspects of the readability assessment problem including reviewing classical readability formulas, presenting several advanced computational approaches based on machine learning techniques and sophisticated linguistic features, and pointing out current interest for readability for specific target populations as well as for texts of peculiar characteristics such as web pages.

2.9   FURTHER READING

Readability formulas and studies have been proposed for many different languages. For Basque, an agglutinative language with rich morphology, Gonzalez-Dios et al. [2014] recently proposed using a number of Basque-specific features to separate documents with two different readability levels, achieving over 90% accuracy (note that is only binary classification). A readability formula developed for Swedish, the *Lix* index, which uses word length and sentence length as difficulty factors, has been used in many other languages [Anderson, 1981]. There has been considerable research on readability in Spanish [Anula Rebollo, 2008, Rodríguez Diéguez et al., 1993, Spaulding, 1956] and its application to automatic text simplification evaluation [Štajner and Saggion, 2013a].

CHAPTER 3

Lexical Simplification

Lexical simplification aims at replacing difficult words with easier-to-read (or understand) expressions while preserving the meaning of the original text segments. For example, the sentence "John composed these verses in 1995" could be lexically simplified into "John wrote the poem in 1995" without altering very much the sense of the initial sentence. Lexical simplification requires the solution of at least two problems: first, finding of a set of synonymic candidates for a given word, generally relying on a dictionary or a lexical ontology and, second, replacing the target word by a synonym which is easier to read and understand in the given context. For the first task, lexical resources such as WordNet [Miller et al., 1990] could be used. For the second task, different strategies of word sense disambiguation (WSD) and simplicity computation are required. A number of works rely on word frequency as a measure of both word complexity and word simplicity [Carroll et al., 1998, Lal and Rüger, 2002], others argue that length is a word complexity factor [Bautista et al., 2011], while some use a combination of frequency and length [Bott et al., 2012a, Keskisärkkä, 2012].

This chapter starts with the first approach to lexical simplification, which relies on WordNet but ignores the ambiguity problem. It then introduces a system for the lexical simplification of Spanish texts which performs word sense dissambiguation using an available synonym dictionary (with word senses) and discrete word vector representations. Then, works to assess the complexity of words in context are reported, in particular in the context of a recent evaluation challenge on complex word identification. Approaches which learn lexical simplification systems using comparable corpora are described, followed by systems which rely on current distributional models of lexical semantics (including continuous word vector representations). The chapter also overviews the lexical simplification challenge which was proposed at SemEval 2012 as an incentive to research on simplicity-based synonym ranking. Finally, a description of a system that simplifies numerical expressions in text is presented.

3.1 A FIRST APPROACH

Carroll et al. [1998] present the first lexical simplifier for English in which each word from an input text is searched for in WordNet [Miller et al., 1990]. A synonym list for each word is created using the WordNet lexical database and the Oxford Psycholinguistic Database (Kučera-Francis frequency list) [Quinlan, 1992] is queried to find the synonyms' frequencies in order to proceed to replace the word with its most frequent synonym. As an example consider the text: "My automobile is broken," the word "automobile" has as synonyms "car," "auto," "machine," and "motorcar" which have the following counts in the Kučera-Francis frequency count list: car (278), auto (26), machine (108), motorcar (0), automobile (50). Therefore, the word "car" is the easier synonym of "automobile" being therefore selected as a replacement of "automobile" resulting in the sentence "My car is broken." It is worth noting that this approach does not take word sense disambiguation into consideration; however, the authors argue that, in practice, this is not a problem since infrequent words tend to have a very specific meaning and thus no word sense disambiguation is required.

The approach was further explored by Shardlow [2014], who implemented and evaluated the above procedure analyzing possible sources of errors during lexical simplification. The only minor difference with the original procedure is the selection of words to simplify, which was set to a frequency below five in the Kučera-Francis frequency list. In order to test the approach, a set of 115 news articles from various topics were selected. During the operation of the system, 183 lexical substitutions were identified out of which only 19 were considered correct. The worst type of error was the identification of a word as complex when, according to the evaluator, it did not require to be simplified.

3.2   LEXICAL SIMPLIFICATION IN LEXSIS

LexSiS is a lexical simplification system for Spanish [Bott et al., 2012a, Saggion et al., 2016] which tries to find the best substitution candidate (a word lemma) for every word which has an entry in a lexical database. The substitution operates in two steps: first the system tries to find the most appropriate substitution set, i.e., a list of synonyms, for a given word, and then it tries to find the best substitution candidate within this set, where the best substitution is one which satisfies a simplicity criterion.

The lexical database adopted by LexSiS is the Spanish Open Thesaurus (SOT) which lists 21,831 target words (lemmas) and provides a list of word senses for each word. Each word sense is, in turn, a list of substitute words. For example, the word *luchador* (fighter) has seven entries or senses in the SOT. One such entry contains the list of synonyms *boxeador, pugilista, etc.*, corresponding to the literal meaning of the word fighter (i.e., boxer), another entry contains the list of synonyms *perseverante, tenaz, etc.*, corresponding to the figurative sense of the word (i.e., resolute).

In a nutshell, the procedure for simplifying the vocabulary is as follows: for each lemma in the text that is considered a complex word, a word vector is created considering the context of the word. This vector is compared to all available sense vectors of the lemma in the thesaurus to pick the closest vector, and then from the list of synonym words which also includes the target word, the best substitute is selected.

In order to measure lexical similarity between words and word contexts, a word vector space model [Sahlgren, 2006], which represents words in very local contexts, is used. In this model, the "meaning" of a word is represented as the contexts in which the word can be found. A word vector can be extracted from contexts observed in a corpus, where the dimensions represent the words in the context, and the component values represent their frequencies. The similarity between two words can be measured in terms of their vectors' cosine similarity. Word senses are also represented as vectors in LexSiS. The word vectors of all synonyms for a given word sense are added to yield a sense vector. The word vector model has to be trained on a large corpus. For LexSiS, this was done on an 8-million-word corpus of Spanish online news. The vectors contained lemmas occurring in a nine-word window of the target word with stop-words removed. Where word sense disambiguation is concerned, two different methods to select a suitable word sense are used in LexSiS: the local method looks at the local context of a target word, assuming that the local context provides enough information for disambiguation [Krovetz, 1998], while a global method takes all the occurrences of the target word within a text and constructs a combined representation of the contexts in which they are found, assuming the one-sense-per-discourse hypothesis [Gale et al., 1992]. In any case, the vectors will contain lemmas and counts and will be rather sparse.

Based on a corpus study on frequency and length distribution in the Simplext corpus (see Section 8.4), LexSiS uses a simplicity measure combination of word length and word frequency (see Bott et al. [2012a] for details concerning the simplicity function).

There are several cases when LexSiS will not substitute the target word, including cases where the target word is already very frequent or when the chosen replacement is too different from the target word (measured using the vector similarity between the words) or when the replacement does not fit very well in the current text context (also measured as the similarity with the target vector).

LexSiS was evaluated using answers to multiple-choice questionnaires administered to three Spanish speakers. The questionnaires included a sentence with a target word and the same sentence with the target word substituted (no information about the source was given). Substitutions were generated using gold substitutions, substitutions by a baseline frequency algorithm (similar to Carroll et al. [1998], see above), and substitutions by LexSiS. Examples of sentences presented to the participants are as follows:

- Original: *Descubren en Valencia una nueva ESPECIE de pez prehitórico.* (A new SPECIES of prehistoric fish is discovered in Valencia.)

- LexSiS: *Descubren en Valencia un nuevo TIPO de pez prehitórico.* (A new TYPE of prehistoric fish is discovered in Valencia.)

- Frequency: *Descubren en Valencia un nuevo GRUPO de pez prehitórico.* (A new GROUP of prehistoric fish is discovered in Valencia.)

For each pair of sentences A and B, the participants had to answer how sentence B was with respect to A: "simpler," "more complex," "same complexity," "don't have same meaning," "don't understand." Overall, LexSiS produced more synonym substitutions than the frequency-based method (over 72% for LexSiS compared to just over 66% for frequency), and from those cases where LexSiS produced a synonym, in most cases the synonym was simpler than or equally complex as the original.

3.3   ASSESSING WORD DIFFICULTY

Shardlow [2013] compares different techniques to identify complex words (CW) in English. Common techniques for CW identification include frequency thresholding. In his work, a corpus of CW examples is created based on edit histories from Simple Wikipedia. Aligned pairs of sentences $(XwY, X\overline{w}Y)$ with exactly one replacement (w by $\overline{w}$) are extracted from a Simple Wikipedia edit history and word w annotated as complex in the given context. In order to provide negative examples, one word per sentence is picked at random from the sentence and annotated as a negative example, keeping the dataset balanced in terms of positive and negative examples. Three methods are tested for classifying CW: the first method is the implementation of Carroll et al. [1998] seen before, and another method uses a frequency threshold (i.e., a word whose frequency is below a threshold is considered CW) learned from a corpus by using a 5-fold cross-validation procedure. The third method uses a SVM to train an algorithm that uses only word features to decide on its complexity, which means that no context is used to inform the classifier. All methods perform similarly in terms of F1. In the following paragraphs we will show approaches that use contextual information to decide on the complexity of a word.

With the objective of promoting the development of systems able to, given a sentence and a target word, decide whether the word is complex or not, the Complex Word Identification task [Paetzold and Specia, 2016a] was proposed. The dataset prepared for the task is a set of 9,200 sentences extracted from the CW corpus [Shardlow, 2013], the LexMturk corpus [Horn et al., 2014], and Simple English Wikipedia [Kauchak, 2013]. A sample of 200 sentences was annotated by 20 subjects (non-native English speakers). In the annotation process, for each word (noun, verb, adjective, or adverb) the subjects had to indicate whether they could not understand it, even if they could understand the overall meaning of the sentence. The rest of the sentences (9,000) were annotated by just one subject. Based on this data, two training sets were created: the optimistic training set labels as complex those words which were identified as complex by at least one subject; the conservative dataset considers complex those words judged as difficult by at least five subjects. Twenty teams submitted systems for the complex word identification task and were evaluated in terms of precision, recall, accuracy, F-score, and G-score which is the harmonic mean between accuracy and recall. The task organizers indicate that in terms of G-score the two best teams were the organizers themselves [Paetzold and Specia, 2016b] and the TALN team [Ronzano et al., 2016]. The task organizers prepared a system which relies on a voting schema (e.g., ensemble methods) using 23 different systems and a total of 69 distinct morphological, lexical, semantic, collocation-based, and nominal features. Using cross-validation over the training data, they selected how many of the top systems to combine and used the system confidence over a validation dataset to weight systems responses. The TALN team developed a trainable approach based on Random Forest classifiers. Several features were implemented, including the frequency of both the word and the surrounding ones computed in several corpora, the position of the word in the sentence, the depth of the word in the dependency tree of the sentence, the presence of the word in simple/complex word lists and several measures computed by relying on WordNet [Miller et al., 1990], and the results of Word Sense Disambiguation [Agirre and Soroa, 2009] applied to sentences. The method also used a weighting mechanism so that the number of annotators that considered the word as complex is taken into account during training. In terms of F-score the best two teams were Wrobel [2016] and Malmasi et al. [2016]. The system by Wrobel [2016], which obtained the highest F-score, used document frequency over Simple English Wikipedia: if the word's frequency was below some threshold, the word was classified as complex, where the threshold was optimized to achieve optimal F-score. The system by Malmasi et al. [2016] uses the target word to estimate several probabilities from corpora: the probability of the word itself, the probability of the word given (conditioned to) the preceding words (up to two words), and the joint probabilities of the word in several contexts. They also used a word length feature. Their classifier was based on decision-trees ensemble methods where each decision tree was trained on different versions of the training dataset.

3.4   USING COMPARABLE CORPORA

Recently, the availability of the Simple English Wikipedia (SEW) [Coster and Kauchak, 2011], in combination with the "ordinary" English Wikipedia (EW), made a new generation of text simplification approaches possible, which use primarily machine learning techniques [Coster and Kauchak, 2011, Wubben et al., 2012, Zhu et al., 2010].

3.4.1   USING SIMPLE ENGLISH WIKIPEDIA EDIT HISTORY

Yatskar et al. [2010] use edit histories from the SEW to identify pairs of possible synonyms and the combination of SEW and EW in order to create a set of lexical substitution rules of the form $x \rightarrow y$. Given a pair of edit histories eh_1 and eh_2, they identify which words from eh_1 have been replaced in order to make eh_2 "simpler" than eh_1. A probabilistic approach is used to model the likelihood of a replacement of word x by word y being made because y is "simpler." In order to estimate the parameters of the model, various assumptions are made, such as whether word replacement in SEW is due to simplification or normal editing and that the frequency of edits in SEW is proportional to that of edits in EW. In their evaluation, subjects are presented with substitution pairs $(x \rightarrow y)$ obtained using different methods including a human-made dictionary of substitutions and random and frequency-based baselines obtained from all possible substitution pairs. Subjects are asked to evaluate how x is when compared to y—more simple, more complex, equally simple/complex, not a synonym, or "undecided." Although the proposed approach performs worse than the dictionary, it is better than the two baselines.

3.4.2   USING WIKIPEDIA AND SIMPLE WIKIPEDIA

Biran et al. [2011] also rely on the SEW/EW combination without paying attention to the edit history of the SEW. They use context vectors to identify pairs of words which occur in similar contexts in SEW and EW (using cosine similarity). WordNet is used as a filter for possible lexical substitution rules $(x \rightarrow y)$. In this approach, a word complexity measure is defined which takes into account word length and word frequency. Given a pair of "synonym" words (w_1, w_2), their raw frequencies are computed on SEW ($\text{freq}_{sew}(w_i)$) and EW ($\text{freq}_{ew}(w_i)$). A complexity score for each word is then computed as the ratio between its EW and SEW frequencies (i.e., $\text{complexity}(w) = \text{freq}_{ew}(w) / \text{freq}_{sew}(w)$). The final word complexity combines the frequency complexity factor with the length factor in the following formula: $\text{final\_complexity}(w) = \text{complexity}(w) * \text{len}(w)$. As an example, for the word pair (*canine*, *dog*) the following inequality will hold: $\text{final\_complexity}(canine) > \text{final\_complexity}(dog)$. This indicates that *canine* could be replaced by *dog* but not vice versa. During text simplification, Biran et al. use a *context-aware* method comparing how well the substitute word fits the context, filtering out possibly harmful rule applications which would select word substitutes with the wrong word sense. Their approach is similar to the one used in LexSiS in that they use a vector space model to capture lexical semantics and, with that, context preferences.

Horn et al. [2014] cast simple synonym candidate selection as a ranking problem and train a SVM ranking procedure using manual annotated data collected using Amazon's Mechanical Turk. Their approach improves over the above rule-based system. Here, synonyms for each word are extracted from phrase alignment tables learned from aligned sentences from EW and SEW using GIZA++ [Och and Ney, 2003]. The features used for representing synonyms in a given context include word frequency from several sources, phrase alignment probabilities, language model likelihood, etc. There is a recent tendency to use statistical machine translation techniques for text simplification that are covered in Chapter 5. In this case, lexical simplification is treated as an implicit part of the machine translation problem where mixed lexical and (very limited) syntactical simplifications are learned at the same time.

3.5 LANGUAGE MODELING FOR LEXICAL SIMPLIFICATION

The lexical simplification approach of De Belder et al. [2010] uses two sources of information: (i) a dictionary of synonyms and (ii) a latent words language model (LWLM), which, given a large corpus, learns for each word a set of synonyms and related words. LWLM provides a way to perform word sense disambiguation or filtering (i.e., words suggested by the LWLM can be ignored if they are not found in an authoritative list of synonyms). In order to select the simpler synonym of a word in context, a probabilistic approach is proposed where two sources of information are combined: on the one hand, information from the LWLM (i.e., suitability of the synonym in the given context) and, on the other hand, the probability that the synonym is "easy." The authors argue that the later probability can be estimated from a psycholinguistic database mapping frequencies to values to the interval $[0, 1]$ or could be unigram probabilities estimated from a corpus written in "simple" language such as the ESW.

Glavaš and Štajner [2015] propose a simplification method based on current distributional lexical semantics approaches [Pennington et al., 2014]. They argue that simplification approaches depend on the availability of corpora or lexical resources which may be unavailable in some cases. Although they do not rely on lexical resources, they do use available corpora (English Wikipedia and the Gigaword 5 corpora[1]) since they model word semantics using pre-trained word vectors from GloVe [Pennington et al., 2014], a state-of-the art tool for lexical semantics modeling. The approach which the authors call LIGHT-LS is simple. Given a target word w they extract from the word embedding model the words v whose vectors are closer in terms of cosine similarity with the vector of w. The generated words are then ranked based on the following criteria: semantic similarity (the cosine similarity with the target word), context similarity (the average cosine similarity with the context of target word in the text), the information content of the candidate compared to that of the target, and the fitness of the candidate substitute in context (measured with the likelihood of a 5-gram language model). The evaluation is performed on the LexMturk corpus [Horn et al., 2014] and on the dataset produced for the SemEval lexical simplification task [Specia et al., 2012] (see Section 3.6). On the LexMturk dataset the evaluation is assessed with the metrics precision, accuracy, and the percentage of words changed by the system. LIGHT-LS shows better performance in terms of accuracy and percent of changes produced. On the lexical simplification task, the approach outperforms the best system in the task [Jauhar and Specia, 2012]. However, the approach is not without limitations: in human assessment of the simplified output, the system shows less meaning preservation capabilities than the other evaluated systems, due to the fact of LIGHT-LS being unable to discern between synonyms and antonyms, thus casting doubt on the idea of not considering lexical resources in the approach.

Paetzold [2016] also relies on current word embedding representations for the task of substitute generation but using POS annotated corpora to create his word representations where universal POS tags are used for verbs, nouns, adjectives, and adverbs. The author argues that by joint modeling words and POS tags, a substitute generation algorithm would effectively filter out words which do not share the same POS tag as the target word. As shown by Mikolov et al. [2013], embedding models are able to capture synonymy. However these models are also prone to relate words with their antonyms; for example, a word such as *good* will be similar to *decent* and *nice* but also to *bad*. Following the method proposed by Faruqui et al. [2015] to modify the embeddings of a word (retrofitting) so that it will have shorter distances with words that share a certain relation with it such as synonymy, hypernymy, or hyponymy, Paetzold uses WordNet, which encodes POS tags compatible with the ones he uses. Considering all pairs of synonyms in WordNet, he creates a retrofitted model using the word2vec toolkit,[2] training the model on a corpus of about 7 billion words. Given a target word together with its POS tag, substitutes are generated from the retrofitted model by considering the ten top words (greatest cosine similarity) with the given word and POS tag. In an evaluation in which the LexMturk corpus [Horn et al., 2014] is used, performance is measured with the traditional metrics precision, recall, and F-measure and also with potential—the proportion of generated instances which are present in

---

[1]https://catalog.ldc.upenn.edu/LDC2011T07
[2]https://code.google.com/archive/p/word2vec/

the gold standard substitutions. The retrofitted substitution generation performs favorably when compared with other competitive approaches such as those by Biran et al. [2011] and Kauchak [2013].

3.6   LEXICAL SIMPLIFICATION CHALLENGE

A lexical simplification task was proposed in the SemEval evaluation [Specia et al., 2012], where given a word and a set of possible substitutes, the automatic systems have to identify the simpler synonym(s). More specifically, the goal of the English Lexical Simplification task was to rank (by lexical simplicity) several synonyms for a target word in a context. The dataset for this task, which was derived from the English Lexical Substitution Task dataset [McCarthy and Navigli, 2009], has 2,010 contexts which are divided into trial and test sets, consisting of 300 and 1710 contexts respectively. The dataset covers a total of 201 words of the following types: nouns, verbs, adverbs, and adjectives. Each word is shown in 10 different contexts. An example is shown in Figure 3.1 where a sentence is shown with a word to be simplified—*bright*. The set of possible substitutes is provided, that are grouped by simplicity and sorted from simplest to most complex.

Original sentence: During the siege, George Robertson had appointed Shujaul-Mulk, who was a *bright* boy only 12 years old and the youngest surviving son of Aman-ul-Mulk, as the ruler of Chitral.

Set of possible substitutes: intelligent; bright; clever; smart

Simplicity Gold Rankings (average of human annotators): {intelligent} {clever} {smart} {bright}

Figure 3.1: Example of the SemEval 2012 English lexical simplification task.

The gold rankings for synonyms in context were generated by averaging the ranking given by human annotators (four people for the training set and three people for the test set) to the set of synonyms. The task considered three baseline systems: a system that uses the best substitution (not simpler) in context, a random system, and a frequency-based substitution procedure (as in Carroll et al. [1998] using frequencies from the Google Web IT Corpus [Brants and Franz, 2006]). The challenge was taken by five research sites, which submitted one or more systems for evaluation. The evaluation measure used to assess systems' output was an adaptation of the kappa index for pairwise rank comparison by Callison-Burch et al. [2011]. Only one of the participating systems [Jauhar and Specia, 2012] was able to beat the hard-to-beat frequency-based simplifier by a small margin, demonstrating the complexity of the task.

3.7   SIMPLIFYING NUMERICAL EXPRESSIONS IN TEXT

One type of information which is omnipresent in human communication is numerical information, which can pose comprehension problems for different types of readers. In fact, at a certain age, it might be easier to understand a ratio ("one fourth") than a percentage ("25%") or, at any stage, an approximate number ("almost 1 million people") easier to read than an exact number ("1,999,708 persons") or a digit ("9") easier to recognize in written form than a word ("nine"). Also, knowing that the "distance between Madrid and Barcelona is exactly 504.64 km" may be unnecessary in some situations and knowing that Barcelona is "about 500 km" from Madrid could suffice.

Bautista and Saggion [2014] propose an approach to simplifying numerical expressions in Spanish texts using a set of text re-writing strategies drawn from the analysis of a corpus (see Section 8.4) and a survey. Examples of typical cases of simplification are shown in Table 3.1.

Table 3.1: Simplification of numerical expressions in text

Cerca de 1,9 millones de personas asistieron al concierto (About 1.9 million people attended the concert)	Casi 2 millones de personas asistieron al concierto (Nearly 2 million people attended the concert)
Sólo se ha vendido un cuarto de las entradas (Only a quarter of the tickets have been sold)	Sólo se ha vendido 1/4 de las entradas (Only 1/4 of the tickets have been sold)
Uno de cada cuatro niños hablan chino (One in four children speak Chinese)	1 de cada 4 niños hablan chino (1 in 4 children speak Chinese)
Asistieron un 57% de la clase (57% of the class attended)	Asistieron mas de la mitad de la clase (More than half of the class attended)
Aprobaron el 98% (98% passed)	Aprobaron casi todos (Almost everyone passed)

The simplification procedure proposed has the following steps:

- a Spanish text analysis tool is used to sentence split, tokenize, and part-of-speech tag the texts [Padró et al., 2010];

- a set of grammars is applied to the text in order to identify extended numerical expressions;

- simplification rules are applied to the identified numerical expressions; and

- sentences are rewritten with the original numerical expressions modified.

The most important aspect of the text analysis tool is that it recognizes quite complex numerical expressions in Spanish which are tagged with a "Z" tags (for example an expression such as "16,4 milliones" (16.4 million) will be tagged with the "Zd" tag). The second component is a named entity recognition grammar with 45 rules implemented in the Java Annotation Pattern Engine (JAPE) language [Cunningham et al., 2000]. The main objective of this component is to target "Z" tags in order to create more complete numerical expressions which will include modifiers such as "alrededor de 3952 millones de años" (about 3952 million years). A set of rewriting strategies were discovered in the corpus and by analyzing the answers to a questionnaire where Spanish speakers were asked to replace numerical expressions in context by simpler expressions. One rewriting strategy consists, for example, in rounding the value of the numerical expression and adding a modifier to indicate the loss of precision ("3.9 million people" simplified into "almost 4 million people"). The rewriting program has been implemented in Java using a mathematical library to manipulate the numerical transformations. The approach was rather positively evaluated in the integrated Simplext software (see Section 6.2.3). However many questions remain, notably, the semantics and pragmatics of the original numerical expression are not considered. If the numerical expression is meant as an exact number which should not be modified or if manipulation of the number affects the meaning of the text, these operations should probably be avoided. Consider for example the following case "UK inflation rose from 1.2% in September to 1.3% in October," transforming it into "UK inflation rose from just over 1% in September to just over 1% in October" would be rather inappropriate because of the meaningless resulting text.

3.8   CONCLUSION

Lexical simplification, the task of modifying the vocabulary of the text by choosing words which make the text easier to read and understand by a target population, is a complicated task which requires a great deal of lexical and world knowledge. First, it is necessary to detect what words may cause problems to the reader of the text and, to do so, internal as well as external evidence may be required (e.g., word frequency, age-of-acquisition or ambiguity information). Second, it is necessary to have an inventory of suitable substitutes for a given word, which may be obtained from carefully handcrafted databases (e.g., WordNet) or automatically induced from comparable corpora. Finally, a method is required to select the best substitute in a given context, a substitute with the same meaning, which is simpler for the user. The target user is fundamental in understanding what words should be replaced and what words should be used as substitutes, since different words may be more or less appropriate for him/her. Most techniques in use today rely on simple surrogates (e.g., frequency) of word simplicity/complexity and available dictionaries, which might be insufficient to provide enough coverage. Lexical simplification has usually been treated as a word-by-word substitution task where little attention is paid to the effects a synonym substitution may cause in the overall cohesion and coherence of the text. By proceeding on a word-by-word basis, systems also ignore complex linguistic phenomena such as collocations and multi-word-expressions, which should be dealt with in appropriate ways during simplification.

3.9   FURTHER READING

Many questions worth investigating remain open in automatic lexical simplification. Lexical simplification methods usually use the local context of words and phrases disregarding cohesion and coherence, which are essential properties of a text. Since a text is a set of interconnected units, substitutions of one lexical unit by another may considerably change text properties such as its intended meaning, cohesion, and coherence. There are many word properties worth investigating in the context of lexical simplification. For example, Walker et al. [2011] studied the role of ambiguity in a lexical substitution task noting that when a synonym has to be selected for a given word, readers rank less ambiguous/less common synonyms higher than more ambiguous/more common synonyms. This could also be an interesting topic to investigate in lexical simplification. Health information is a very relevant field for the application of lexical simplification technology. Medical information is notoriously difficult because of the presence of medical terminology and abbreviations which may impede lay reader's comprehension [Keselman et al., 2007]; therefore, lexical simplification seems particularly relevant in this specific field. Zeng-Treitler et al. [2007], for example, present an explanation generation system in the field of personal health records. In a similar domain, Elhadad [2006] investigates word familiarity prediction and how to define unfamiliar terms in clinical studies. Finally, the reader is referred to Paetzold [2016] for a pipelined approach to lexical simplification, which is composed, in sequence, of (i) complex word identification; (ii) substitution generation; (iii) substitution selection; and (iv) substitution ranking.

CHAPTER 4

Syntactic Simplification

Syntactic simplification aims at transforming long sentences containing syntactic phenomena which may hinder readability for certain people into simpler paraphrases which do not contain those phenomena. Examples of syntactic structures which may be perceived as complicated are subordination, coordination, relative clauses, and sentences which do not follow the cannonical word order. In this chapter, an overview of past and current rule-based systems will be presented. The development of rule-based systems generally requires linguistic expertise, resulting in very precise systems which will nonetheless suffer from lack of coverage. They will also underperform if the accuracy of parsers or taggers, which are needed to analyze the input sentence, is suboptimal. The advantage of these systems, however, is that they do not require large annotated corpora to be developed. In the next chapter, systems that learn simplification from corpora will be outlined. The chapter starts with the first rule-based approach to syntactic simplification, to then overview work on problems related to sentence order and word choice which need to be addressed when generating texts. A full rule-based simplification system and two approaches which rely on information extraction and generation are also outlined.

4.1 FIRST STEPS IN SYNTACTIC SIMPLIFICATION

Syntactic simplification was introduced by Chandrasekar et al. [1996], who developed a rule-based approach to transform sentences so that they could be correctly parsed by automatic syntactic analysers. Their approach targeted constructions such as relative clauses and appositions, providing the foundation for current rule-based simplification approaches. An example of a rule to deal with relative clauses constructions is:

$$WX : NP, RELPRONY, Z. \rightarrow WX : NPZ.X : NPY.$$

which could transform (1) into (2):

(1) Hu Jintao, who is the current Paramount Leader of the People's Republic of China, was visiting Spain.

(2) Hu Jintao was visiting Spain. Hu Jintao is the current Paramount Leader of the People's Republic of China.

By matching variables in the left-hand side of the rule as follows: W = "", X = "Hu Jintao," Y = "is the current Paramount Leader of the People's Republic of China" and, Z = "was visiting Spain" and rewriting the sentence using the pattern in the right-hand side of the rule.

Acknowledging that handcrafting simplification rules is time consuming, Chandrasekar and Srinivas [1997] propose learning rules automatically from parallel data. Pairs of original and simplified sentences were parsed using a Lightweight Dependency Analyzer [Srinivas, 1997]; the resulting analysis is then chunked to combine elements creating a coarse-grained analysis. The sentences are compared with a tree-comparison algorithm in order to identify transformations required to convert the input tree into the output tree. The transformations include variables which are instantiated using a constraint satisfaction mechanism. Rules are then generalized, changing specific words to tags. The training set for learning rules was rather small with only 65 texts.

An example of the kind of data used to learn is presented in Figures 4.1 and 4.2 where the representations of original ("Talwinder Singh, who masterminded the 1984 Kanishka crash, was killed in a fierce two-hour encounter.") and simplified sentences ("Talwinder Singh was killed in a fierce two-hour encounter. Talwinder Singh masterminded the 1984 Kanishka crash.") represented as chunks and dependencies are shown. The approach was only attempted to induce rules for simplification of relative clauses. In spite of this early attempt to learn text simplification rules from data, syntactic simplification research continued with handcrafted rule-based systems. In fact, the limitations at the time were obvious; although the rules were not manually created, the data was (a handful of examples). It was also too limited to scale up.

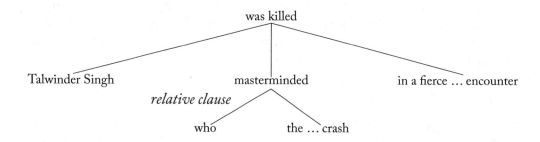

Figure 4.1: A complex sentence (containing a relative clause) represented as a kind of dependency tree.

4.2   SYNTACTIC SIMPLIFICATION AND COHESION

Siddharthan [2006] is also in favor of rule-based systems, but he is mainly concerned with text generation issues in text simplification such as ordering of the simplified sentences, word choice, generation of referring expressions, and choice of determiner, which were not treated by previous rule-based approaches. In fact, he argues that blind application of some simplification rules can damage text cohesion, as in the following example where sentence (1) which contains a conjunction and a relative clause is transformed into a sequence of three much simpler sentences (2a), (2b), and (2c).

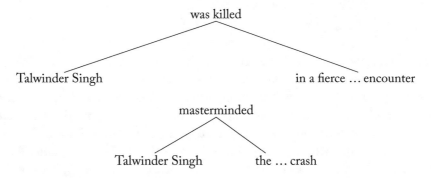

Figure 4.2: Two simple sentences equivalent to the sentence in Figure 4.1 (without a relative clause).

(1) Mr. Anthony, who runs an employment agency, decries program trading, but he isn't sure it should be strictly regulated.

(2a) Mr. Anthony decries program trading. (2b) Mr. Anthony runs an employment agency. (2c) But he isn't sure it should be strictly regulated.

Siddarthan argues that this transformation badly affects text cohesion since the adversative clause (2c) is now linked to sentence (2b) instead of to (2a) as it should be. Note that the pronoun "it" could also be misinterpreted as referring to the "employment agency." To deal with these problems, a three-stage architecture composed of analysis, transformation, and regeneration is proposed [Siddharthan, 2002]. In the actual implementation of the architecture, analysis is only superficial (i.e., noun and verb chunking) because the parsers of that time were subject to time out. Issues such as clause attachment are dealt with through specific procedures relying on machine learning, prepositional preferences, and WordNet hierarchies.

A set of transformation rules—the transformation stage—is in charge of identifying syntactic patterns and proposing transformations. Seven rules are used to deal with conjunction, relative clauses, and oppositions. Rules are applied recursively until no more transformations are possible. The regeneration stage is in charge of handling conjunctive cohesion (this is done during transformation) and anaphoric cohesion.

Sentence ordering is dealt with locally (whenever a pair of new simpler sentences is created out of a complex one) as a constraint satisfaction problem where constraints are introduced by rhetorical relations appearing in the original sentence which must be preserved in the simplified version. Constraints specify local order based on type of relation and where the nuclei of the transformed sentences should be generated. In order to render rhetorical relations simply, fixed cue-words are chosen; for example, a concession will always be generated using "but". Pronouns are replaced only when a pronominal resolution algorithm returns different antecedents for original and simplified texts.

4.3   RULE-BASED SYNTACTIC SIMPLIFICATION USING SYNTACTIC DEPENDENCIES

Siddharthan [2011] uses typed dependency representations from the Stanford Parser, arguing that typed dependencies represent a high level of abstraction, thus allowing for easy writing of rules and for their automatic acquisition from corpora. Manually developed rules are used to transform into simpler sentences an input containing the following syntactic phenomena: coordination, subordination, apposition, passive constructions, and relative clauses. The transformation rules are implemented with two types of operations: delete and insert. Siddharthan explains how activization of the sentence in the passive voice "The cat was chased by the dog." is carried out. The transformation is modeled as three delete operations and two insert operations as shown in Figure 4.3. **Match** and **delete** operations are used to eliminate tuples from the representation which are substituted by elements introduced by **insert** operations.

Input sentence (with positions)

The$_1$ cat$_2$ was$_3$ chased$_4$ by$_5$ the$_6$ dog$_7$.$_8$

Representation with typed dependencies

det(cat-2; The-1)
nsubjpass(chased-4, cat-2)
auxpass(chased-4, was-3)
det(dog-7, the-6)
agent(chased-4, dog-7)
punct(chased-4, .-8)

Match and Delete Rules

nsubjpass(??X0, ??X1)
auxpass(??X0, ??X2)
agent(??X0, ??X3)

Insert Rules

nsubj(??X0, ??X3)
dobj(??X0, ??X1)

Output sentence(s)

The dog chased the cat.

Figure 4.3: Simplification rules over typed-dependencies.

Siddharthan argues that original word order could generally be used for generation—in-order dependency tree traversal—but not always. For example, for activization of passive constructions as in the example above, the generation process would invert the normal (in-order) tree traversal. Also, while the surface words from the original sentence could in many cases be re-used for generation, there will be situations when this is not possible, since agreement between, for example, subject and verb is required. Therefore, rules to extract agreement features from the dependency representation are also added to the representation. The transformed representation is used to generate sentences using two approaches: a statistical generator and a rule-based generation system. The rule-based generator uses the original words and original word order, except when lexical rules and explicit order indication are included in the representation. The statistical generator is an off-the-shelf system, RealPro [Lavoie and Rambow, 1997], which uses as input Deep Syntactic Structures (DSSs) [Mel'čuk, 1988]. In order to use the RealPro realizer, a set of transformation procedures is implemented to map typed-dependencies into DSSs. Since parse errors cause infelicitous simplified sentences, Siddharthan proposes to use the n-best parses to overgenerate and select the best simplifications out of them; the selection criteria are based on negative points for sentences containing consecutive word repetition, ending on pronouns or prepositions, etc. and positive points for sentences containing bigrams or trigrams overlapping with the input sentence, etc. Evaluation of the approach looks at the extent of the simplification achieved and the precision with which rules where applied. In general, overgenerating and ranking is proved to be a good strategy to cope with ill-parsed sentences.

Siddharthan later extends the approach [Siddharthan and Mandya, 2014] to include the possibility of automatically learning local transformations using Synchronous Dependency Insertion Grammars [Ding and Palmer, 2005]. This addition makes it possible to better model lexical transformations, which were scarcely covered in the initial system. Comparison against a fully supervised approach [Woodsend and Lapata, 2011] shows the superiority of a hybrid system: indeed, linguistic knoweldge is important to cover real phenomena even without examples in the training corpus.

4.4   PATTERN MATCHING OVER DEPENDENCIES WITH JAPE

In the context of the project *Able to Include* [Saggion et al., 2015a], Ferrés et al. [2015, 2016] present a linguistically motivated syntactic simplification system for English. The system is based on a set of rules which perform pattern matching on the output of a dependency-based parser and a set of re-writing programs in charge of generating the actual simplification. The syntactic phenomena targeted by the system correspond to those identified in previous research as obstacles to readability and understanding [Siddharthan, 2002] and are as follows.

- Passive constructions

	Complex: The release **was accompanied by** a number of TV appearances, including a full hour on On the Record.

	Simple: A number of TV appearances, including a full hour on On the Record **accompanied** the release.

- Appositive constructions

	Complex: The moon is named after **Portia, the heroine of William Shakespeare's play The Merchant of Venice.**

	Simple: The moon is named after Portia. **Portia is the heroine of William Shakespeare's play The Merchant of Venice.**

- Relative clauses

	Complex: The festival was held in **New Orleans, which was recovering from Hurricane Katrina.**

	Simple: The festival was held in New Orleans. **New Orleans was recovering from Hurricane Katrina.**

- Coordinated constructions

	Complex: Tracy **killed** 71 people, **caused** $837 million in damage and **destroyed** more than 70 percent of Darwin's buildings, including 80 percent of the houses.

	Simple: Tracy **killed** 71 people. Tracy **caused** $837 million in damage. **And** Tracy **destroyed** more than 70 percent of Darwin's buildings, including 80 percent of the houses.

- Correlated correlatives

	Complex: A hypothesis requires more work by the researcher in order to **either** confirm **or** disprove it.

	Simple: A hypothesis **requires** more work by the researcher in order to confirm it. **Or** a hypothesis **requires** more work by the researcher in order to disprove it.

- Subordinate clauses

	Complex: He is perhaps best known for his design for the Natural History Museum in London, **although** he also built a wide variety of other buildings throughout the country.

	Simple: He also built a wide variety of other buildings throughout the country. **But** he is perhaps best known for his design for the Natural History Museum in London.

- Adverbial clauses

    Complex: Oxfordshire is a county in the South East England region, **bordering on** Northamptonshire, Buckinghamshire, Berkshire, Wiltshire, Gloucestershire, and Warwickshire.

    Simple: Oxfordshire is a county in the South East England region. Oxfordshire **borders on** Northamptonshire, Buckinghamshire, Berkshire, Wiltshire, Gloucestershire, and Warwickshire.

The simplification system is a pipeline implemented with four main components: (i) the GATE ANNIE system [Maynard et al., 2002]; (ii) the MATE dependency parser [Bohnet, 2009]; (iii) a set of grammars implemented in JAPE (Java Annotation Pattern Engine) [Cunningham et al., 2000]; and (iv) a set of text-to-text generation programs implemented in Java. The system uses the GATE library and Application Programming Interface (API) [Maynard et al., 2002] to create and manipulate the documents to be simplified. All linguistic information generated by the different programs is added as document annotations (see Maynard et al. [2002]). Two components of the ANNIE system are used: the ANNIE tokenizer segments the text into tokens of different types and the ANNIE sentence splitter segments the text into sentences. Each tokenized sentence is then passed to the MATE dependency parser in textual order to obtain dependency relations. The MATE Parser is a state-of-the-art dependency parser [Bohnet, 2009] which carries out lemmatization, part-of-speech tagging, and dependency parsing. The dependency parser adds a *func* feature to each token in the sentence, representing the dependency relation that holds between the token (the dependent) and its head. A feature also indicates for each token the head it is related to, so as to facilitate dependency-graph traversal.

Rules were manually developed in an iterative process by using dependency-parsed sentences from Wikipedia, which were indexed using the ANNIC system [Aswani et al., 2007]. The process resulted in a set of JAPE rules able to recognize and analyze the different kinds of syntactic phenomena appearing in the sentences (those stated above). Each rule is composed of a left-hand side (LHS) and a right-hand side (RHS). The LHS of a rule consists of an annotation pattern description while the RHS consists of annotation manipulation statements. Annotations matched on the LHS of a rule may be referred to on the RHS by means of labels that are attached to pattern elements. Given the complex problem at hand, it is not enough to perform pattern matching and annotation of the matched elements; the different annotations matched instantiating the pattern have to be properly annotated and related to each other. This process is carried out with Java code in the RHS of each rule. JAPE rules can be organized in grammars which when compiled can be used to perform transduction over annotations based on regular expressions. Each syntactic phenomenon dealt with in the system has a dedicated grammar (i.e., set of rules). These grammars are organized in a main file which specifies the order in which the grammars have to be applied to the text.

The complete rule-based system is composed of: 1 rule for appositive constructions, 17 rules for relative clause identification, 10 rules for coordination of sentences and verb phrases, 4 rules for coordinated correlatives, 8 rules for subordination (concession, cause, etc.), 12 rules for adverbial clauses, and 14 rules for passive constructions. Figure 4.4 shows one of the 17 JAPE rules dealing with relative clauses. Only the regular pattern (LHS) is shown, which will match a dependency-parsed sentence such as the one shown schematically in Figure 4.5.

The result of the rule application can be appreciated in Figure 4.6 (the GATE Graphical User Interface) where the relative clause has been identified together with the antecedent (*Eva*) of the relative pronoun (*whose*).

Such rules together with the Java text-to-text generation programs would produce the simplification *Eva is the daughter of Augustine St. Clare. Eva's real name is Evangeline St. Clare.*

Marimon et al. [2015] report evaluation of the actual simplification rules (for apposition, relative clause, coordination, subordination, and passive). Table 4.1 presents evaluation results in terms of the number of times the grammar was fired, number of times the grammar produced a correct interpretation, number of times the grammar produced an incorrect interpretation, and number of times the grammar did not fire when the phenomena were present in the sentence (i.e., a miss). The evaluation was carried out using 100 previously unseen sentence examples for each syntactic phenomenon considered in the system. As can be appreciated, the system is rather precise although the evaluation is carried out in an optimistic scenario where each grammar was tested on sentences already known to have the phenomenon the grammar should deal with (i.e., the apposition grammar was applied only to sentences known to have appositive constructions).

Table 4.1: Syntactic grammar evaluation

Grammar	Num. Sents.	Fired	Correct	Incorrect	Missed
Appositions	100	100 (100%)	79 (79%)	21 (21%)	0 (0%)
RCs	100	93 (93%)	79 (85%)	14 (15%)	7 (7%)
Coordination	100	62 (62%)	56 (90%)	6 (10%)	38 (38%)
Subordination	100	97 (97%)	72 (74%)	25 (26%)	3 (3%)
Passives	100	91 (91%)	85 (89%)	6 (11%)	9 (9%)

4.5   SIMPLIFYING COMPLEX SENTENCES BY EXTRACTING KEY EVENTS

Instead of preserving the whole sentence material though simplification as in the previously described approaches [Chandrasekar et al., 1996, Ferrés et al., 2015, Siddharthan, 2011], some authors argue for simplification through sentence reduction in order to keep the essential information of the sentence by removing "unnecessary" details [Barlacchi and Tonelli, 2013, Glavaš and Štajner, 2013].

In order to extract the essence of sentences, Glavaš and Štajner [2013] propose an *event-centered* sentence simplification approach which is composed of two main steps: (i) an *event extrac-*

```
Rule: NonRestrRC_SbjPossWh
( ({!Token.category ==~ "(WDT|WP)"})*
({Token}):antecedent_end
):antecedent
(
({Token.string == ","}):rc_start
(({Token.lemma == "whose"}):rprn
( (({Token.category == "RB"})?
{Token.category == "VBN", Token.func == "NMOD"})
| (({Token.category == "RB"} | {Token.category == "JJS"})?
{Token.category == "JJ", Token.func == "NMOD"})
| (({Token.category == "JJ"})? {Token.category == "NN", Token.func == "NMOD"})
)?
{Token.func == "SBJ"})
(({Token.string == ","})?({Token.category == "RB"}|(({Token.category == "IN"} |
{Token.category == "TO"})({Token})+))?({Token.string == ","})?)
({Token.category ==~ "VB([DPZ])?|MD", Token.func == "NMOD"}):rc_hd
):rc
-->
{
// Java Code
....
}
```

Figure 4.4: JAPE regular pattern over dependencies to identify a non-restrictive relative clause with possessive subject.

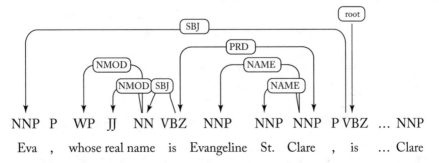

Figure 4.5: Sentence (partial) representation as syntactic dependencies.

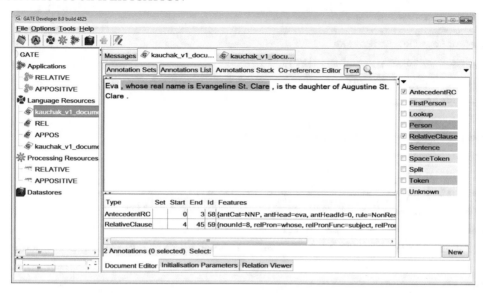

Figure 4.6: JAPE relative clause grammar applied to the sentence *Eva, whose real name is Evangeline St. Clare, is the daughter of Augustine St. Clare.*

tion component, in charge of detecting words which convey the core meaning of events described in a news story; and (ii) a sentence simplification realization component. The event extraction system is a supervised approach which identifies event anchors, i.e., words representing main events, and a rule-based component which identifies arguments of the event anchors. Arguments are *agent*, *target*, *time*, and *location* of given event anchors, which are located and extracted through dependency relations patterns (e.g., nsubj(X, Y)).

Table 4.2 shows two examples of anchors and extracted arguments. In the first example, the verb *confronted* has been identified as an anchor which is related to the word *China* by a subject relation, thus making it possible to extract *China* as the agent of the event (in this case *confront*). The second example has as identified anchor the verb *disputes* which is related to *agreement* by a direct object relation, thus it is extracted as the target of the *dispute* event.

Table 4.2: Two examples of extraction of argument types using dependency patterns

China <u>confronted</u> Philippines	*nsubj* (confront, China)	agent
China <u>disputes</u> **the agreement**	*dobj* (dispute, agreement)	target

Once anchors and arguments have been extracted, two sentence realization components are proposed: in a *sentence-wise* simplification method, words and phrases (e.g., anchors and arguments) not identified by the extraction patterns are removed from the sentence; in an *event-wise* simplification approach, each extracted event (i.e., basically an anchor and its arguments) is used to produce a simple sentence. In this last approach, reporting events are completely ignored, events detected through nominal anchors are also ignored since they are likely to contain few arguments, and gerundive events which govern a main sentence event are transformed into past tense to preserve grammaticality. The generation step just copies the input words to the output sentence, making few transformations, e.g., transforming gerunds into past simple. Table 4.3 shows actual examples of input and output produced by these approaches.

Table 4.3: Examples of sentence-wise and event-wise sentence simplification

Original	Sentence-wise Simplification	Event-wise Simplification
Baset al-Megrahi, the Lybian intelligence officer who was convicted in the 1988 Lockerbie bombing has died at his home in Tripoli, nearly three years after he was released from a Scottish prison.	Baset al-Megrahi was convicted in the 1988 Lockerbie bombing has died at his home after he was released from a Scottish prison.	Baset al-Megrahi was convicted in the 1988 Lockerbie bombing. Baset al-Megrahi has died at his home. Baset al-Megrahi was released from a Scottish prison.

Barlacchi and Tonelli [2013] propose a syntactic sentence simplification system for Italian children's stories. The objective here is to extract from each text factual events (those which have actually occurred in the story), eliminating from them non-mandatory arguments (similar to Glavaš and Štajner [2013]). Text processing is carried out using two main components: an NLP tool for Italian [Pianta et al., 2008] to perform tokenization and lemmatization, and a dependency parser [Lavelli et al., 2009] to produce dependency annotations.

The simplification system is largely rule-based, except for an anaphora resolution component, which was implemented using supervised machine learning. Factual events are extracted looking for verbs, ignoring any verbs in conditional mood or future tense. From the selected verbs, mandatory arguments are extracted using a set of rules, ignoring any non-mandatory arguments. Event reformulation consists of expressing the events in the present tense indicative mood.

Figure 4.7 shows how a sentence might be simplified by the proposed approach. The figure shows that from the input sentence only verb, subject, and direct object are extracted to create the simplification. The main function of the anaphora resolution component mentioned above is to deal with zero-anaphora (i.e., a gap with anaphoric function) so as to recover the omitted subject of a sentence and allow its linguistic realization in the simplified sentence.

4.6 CONCLUSION

Syntactic simplification, concerned with the transformation of long and complicated sentences into shorter simpler ones, requires both syntactic and text generation expertise. Once the sources

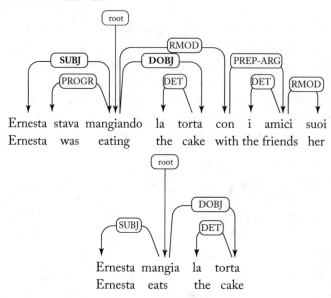

Figure 4.7: Dependency relations of original (*Ernesta stava mangiando la torta con i suoi amici. (Ernesta was eating the cake with their friends.)*) and simplified (*Ernesta mangia la torta. (Ernesta eats the cake.)*) sentences.

of syntactic complexity which affect the target user have been understood from peer-reviewed literature or experimentation, it generally takes an expert linguist to computationally model those phenomena in grammatical terms to be able to recognize them in unseen texts. Both linguistic expertise and corpus analysis would guarantee the development of a broad coverage, precise system. Learning syntactic transformations from corpora is also possible as will be shown in Chapter 5. In addition to the identification of complex syntactic phenomena, which in itself is of great relevance for readability assessment in text simplification (see Chapter 2), once a complex construction has been identified, appropriate transformations need to be performed. These will involve decisions on sentence ordering, noun phrase reformulation, pronoun substitution, etc. Since syntax conveys meaning, it is possible that the intended meaning of the original sentence would be obfuscated by the applied transformation. Syntactic simplification has usually been conceived as a one-size-fits-all solution, with little consideration for simplification systems which can be adapted to the needs of the user.

4.7   FURTHER READING

Related to syntactic simplification is sentence compression, the task of removing from a sentence unimportant details to preserve grammaticality and not greatly affect the meaning of the original. Key approaches to sentence compression include, in addition to rule-based methods [Zajic et al., 2004], the use of *noisy channel models* [Knight and Marcu, 2002] and other optimization techniques [Clarke and Lapata, 2006]. Syntactic paraphrase is clearly related to syntactic simplification; for the interested reader, Dras [1999] identifies several syntactic paraphrases which could be used in text simplification.

CHAPTER 5

Learning to Simplify

Over the last few years the availability of comparable or parallel corpora of original and simplified or adapted textual material has made possible a set of approaches to learn various types of simplification operations from corpora. Notably, with the Simple English Wikipedia (SEW), in combination with the "ordinary" English Wikipedia (EW), simplification approaches which use primarily machine learning techniques have been proposed. Most of them learn lexical changes in the data although some approaches also are able to learn some syntactic transformations. The chapter starts by introducing methods which cast text simplification, in different languages, as monolingual machine translation. Then, we will overview simplification as a statistical syntactic-tree translation process with the aim of transforming complex sentences into simpler ones. We will also overview works which apply optimization techniques aimed at finding the best possible simplification by either optimizing the application of rules or by overgenerating simplification solutions. Finally, to end the chapter we will review recent work on incorporating semantic information into the simplification problem.

5.1 SIMPLIFICATION AS TRANSLATION

Specia [2010] was the first to cast and implement simplification as a kind of machine translation problem where the source sentence, in a complex language, has to be transformed into a sentence in a simple language. She relies on the availability of a corpus of original and simplified sentences produced for the PorSimples project [Aluísio and Gasperin, 2010] (see Section 6.3). The corpus contains two types of simplifications, namely *natural* which are freely produced by annotators, and *strong*, which are produced following specific instructions. Specia uses a standard Statistical Machine Translation (SMT) approach that models the translation of an input sentence f into e using the Bayes Theorem as follows:

$$p(e|f) = \frac{p(f|e)p(e)}{p(f)}, \tag{5.1}$$

where $p(f|e)$ is the probability that a sentence e would be translated into f and $p(e)$ is the probability of sentence e. $p(f)$ is a constant which can be ignored. The key in this model is the phrase-based translation component which decomposes $p(f|e)$ into the product of "phrase translations." Given that multiple translations of a sentence are indeed possible, the method seeks to find a translation e that maximizes a certain probability of being a correct or an acceptable translation. That is:

$$e' = \underset{e \in e*}{\operatorname{argmax}}\, p(f|e)p(e). \tag{5.2}$$

In addition to these probabilities, there are additional parameters to be estimated, such as weights for these models and others that control the ordering of words as well as phrases and the sentence length. The Moses standard phrase-based SMT system [Koehn et al., 2007] is used for training the model using 3,383 pairs of original and simplified sentences and an additional set of 500 pairs for parameter tuning. The model was tested on a set of 500 pairs of aligned sentences. Automatically simplified sentences are compared to human simplifications using the machine translation evaluation metrics BLEU [Papineni et al., 2002] and NIST [Zhang et al., 2004] which both check the overlapping of n-grams between two text units (see Chapter 8 where evaluation metrics are presented). The experiments achieve a BLEU score of 0.6075 and a NIST score of 9.6244. Although BLEU scores of around 0.60 are considered good results in translation, not much can be said about a BLEU score of 0.60 in text simplification. A qualitative analysis of the simplifications shows that the system is rather cautious, since the simplifications are closer to the original sentences than to the reference simplification. Specia also observes that the simplifications, although very simple, are likely to be correct although, on a very few occasions, the automatic simplification is the same as the reference. This work is interesting because of the casting of simplification in a well-established statistical framework. However it should be noted that because of the simple representation adopted (n-gram based), syntactic simplification operations can hardly be captured by the standard SMT model.

5.1.1   LEARNING SIMPLE ENGLISH

Coster and Kauchak [2011] also use an SMT framework to simplify English sentences, training the model with 137,000 aligned pairs of sentences extracted from the traditional English Wikipedia (EW) and the Simple English Wikipedia (SEW) datasets. It is worth noting that sentence pairs in the dataset have similarity above 0.5 using a normalized $tf * idf$ cosine similarity function. They observe that the translation model considers phrases containing one or more words, but phrase deletion and phrase insertion, which are common in simplification, are not implemented. To model deletions, they relax the phrase translation model, explicitly inserting NULLs in the aligned training data. This is done by explicitly aligning any non-aligned word sequences to the string NULL; also, if a sequence $x_1...x_k W y_1...y_l$ aligns to W in the dataset, then x_i and y_i are aligned to NULLs properly inserted in the simplified sentence. Although these transformations may in principle produce undesirable deletion out-of-context, the authors argue the language model can help avoid problematic cases. Where evaluation is concerned, this work significantly extends the previous approach by comparing five different "simplification" approaches, using once again BLEU as an evaluation metric. The approaches compared are: a system which does nothing, two sentence compression approaches, and two MT approaches, namely the unmodified phrase-based translation model and the modified deletion-based model. The compression approaches behave poorly in the simplification task with worse performance than the system that does nothing. Of the two MT-based approaches, the one including deletions is better. By examining the n-best translations and selecting the one which improves the BLEU score, they show that a reranking mechanism could be applied for selection of a more suitable simplification.

Wubben et al. [2012] investigate the SMT approach to simplification even further by incorporating a dissimilarity-based reranking mechanism to chose among possible simplification solutions. The reranking function selects out of the n-best translations produced by the model one which is most different from the original sentence in terms of the Levenshtein edit distance (see Navarro [2001]), which computes the minimum number of insertions, deletions, and substitutions needed to transform one sentence into another. They compared five systems: the gold standard SEW sentence, a baseline word substitution procedure which produces all possible replacements for nouns, adjectives, and verbs in the sentence and selects the solution which highest probability according to a language model trained with SEW, the system described by Zhu et al. [2010] (see below), the sentence simplification system of Woodsend and Lapata [2011], and the SMT system with reranking function. The evaluation of the system is by comparison with state-of-the-art systems using two automatic measures, BLEU and the Flesch-Kincaid grade level, and measuring, relying on human judgment, simplicity (i.e., simpler than the original?), fluency (i.e., grammatical?), and adequacy (i.e., same meaning as the original?) of the simplification using sentences where all systems performed at least one change.

5.1.2 FACING STRONG SIMPLIFICATIONS

Although MT approaches to simplification are interesting from the methodological viewpoint, they still fail to model a number of important operations in text simplification. For example, Štajner [2014] carried out SMT experiments using two different datasets: (i) the Simplext corpus [Saggion et al.] (see Section 8.4) which mainly contains strong simplifications (e.g., semantic paraphrases); and (ii) simplifications of portions of the same corpus without using strong paraphrases. She carried out experiments training two different translation models, one using 700 pairs of strong simplifications and another one using 700 pairs of weak simplifications (similar to what Coster and Kauchak [2011] and Specia [2010] have done). She finds notable differences in BLEU scores depending on the training and testing dataset. While a BLEU score of only 0.0937 is obtained when training and testing on strong simplified data, the BLEU score for the system trained and tested on weak simplifications jumps to 0.4638.

5.2 LEARNING SENTENCE TRANSFORMATIONS

Zhu et al. [2010] consider the syntactic structure of input sentences and cast the problem of sentence simplification as one of finding the best sequence of transformations of a parse tree which will produce the target simplification. Their model assumes that four operations are applied to transform an input parsed sentence into a simplified version: (i) *splitting*; (ii) *dropping*; (iii) *re-*

ordering; and (iv) *substitution*. The splitting operation is responsible for segmenting a tree at a specific split point to obtain two components; usually a relative pronoun would be the split point. The split operation is in fact modeled as two operations: *segmentation* to split the sentence and *completion* to make the sentence complete—replacing a relative pronoun by its antecedent for example. The sentence "August was the sixth month in the ancient Roman calendar which started in 735 BC." shown in Figure 5.1 is transformed into the pair of "sentences" in Figures 5.2 and 5.3 by the application of a split operation (split point is the relative pronoun "which").

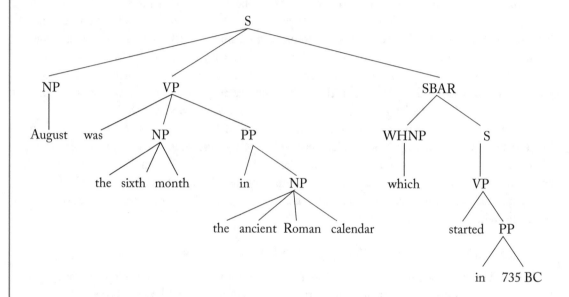

Figure 5.1: Original parsed sentence.

The *dropping* operation will eliminate non-terminal nodes from a parse tree: for example in a **DT JJ NN** (determiner, adjective, noun) noun phrase structure, the adjective (**JJ**) might be deleted. Figure 5.4 shows the result of applying the *dropping* operation to a parse tree (the adjective "Roman" is eliminated).

The *reordering* operation will produce a permutation of the children of a particular node, for example a phrase such as "She has an older brother, Chad and a twin brother" the two conjoined noun phrases may be permuted to get "She has a twin brother and an older brother, Chad."

The final operation, *substitution*, deals with lexical simplification at leaf nodes in the parse tree or at non-terminal nodes in case a full phrase is replaced. Figure 5.5 shows a lexical substitution example where "ancient" is replaced by "old."

The model is probabilistic in that all operations have associated probabilities and the model itself combines all sub-models or probabilities into a translation model. More specifically, if *s* and

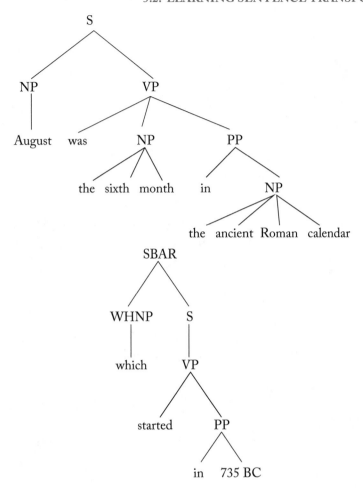

Figure 5.2: Parse-tree after *segmentation*.

c are the simple and complex sentences, the simplification process is modeled as:

$$\mathbf{s} = \underset{s}{\mathrm{argmax}}\, P(s|c)P(s), \tag{5.3}$$

where $P(s|c)$ is a direct translation model and $P(s)$ is a language model for simple sentences. The translation model itself is computed as:

$$P(s|c) = \sum_{\theta:Str(\theta(c))=s} (P(seg|c)P(com|seg)$$

$$\prod_{node} P(dp|node)P(ro|node)P(sub|node)\prod_{w} P(sub|w)), \tag{5.4}$$

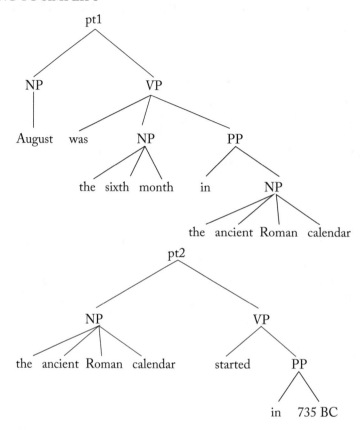

Figure 5.3: Parse-tree after *completion* (replacing relative pronoun by antecedent).

where *seg* is segmentation, *com* is completion, *dp* is drop, *ro* is reorder, and *sub* is substitution and where θ is the sequence of simplification operations applied to the complex sentence c.

A critical aspect of this model is that training data is needed to estimate the probability of application of each operation to parse tree nodes. That is, traces of the transformation of the original sentences are needed. However, it is unknown which transformations were used and in which specific order—there is no such resource available for text simplification research; in fact, there can be many possible ways to transform a sentence or none at all—the simple sentence may be a semantic paraphrase of the complex sentence. Following work by Yamada and Knight [2001] on syntactic-based statistical machine translation, the Expectation Maximization algorithm is used to maximize $P(s|c)$ over a training corpus, where training instances are generated *on the fly* by heuristic application of the simplification operations to the complex sentence until the desired simplified string is obtained.

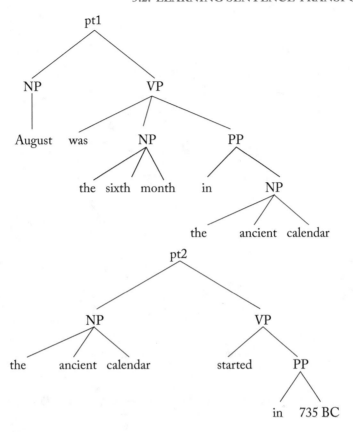

Figure 5.4: Sentences after *deletion*.

Zhu et al.'s model, dubbed TSM, was trained with aligned sentence pairs from English Wikipedia and Simple English Wikipedia known as the PWKP dataset (see Section 8.3 for comments on this dataset). After training, the model was evaluated using an unseen set of 100 complex sentences aligned to 131 simple sentences.

Various algorithms are compared to TSM: (i) a standard statistical machine translation approach (MT) is used and also trained on the PWKP data, using the Moses system [Koehn et al., 2007]; (ii) a sentence compression system (C) [Filippova and Strube, 2008]; (iii) a variant of the sentence compression system enhanced with a lexical simplification procedure (CS); and (iv) an extension of CS with a split procedure that segments the sentence at candidate split points such as relative pronouns and conjuncts (CSS). In addition to the automatic procedures, two types of human data are used: the original complex sentences (CW) and the simple sentences (SW). Table 5.1 shows an example output of the TSM approach.

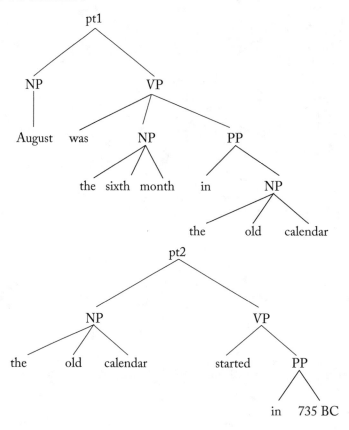

Figure 5.5: Simplified sentences after synonym replacement.

To evaluate the systems, the BLEU score is used to compare systems' output with human written simple sentences (SW). Although the TSM approach obtains a high BLEU score of 0.38, the simple, non-adapted MT approach obtains an even higher score of 0.55. All the other systems perform worse than the translation approaches. However, it is worth noting that the MT output is very close to CW sentences in terms of BLEU (0.78), indicating that very little simplification is actually carried out. In a readability assessment evaluation using the Flesch and Lix readability scores, the TMS approach is the best performing method. However, this result should be taken cautiously, since a very crude splitting procedure such as the one used by the CSS approach, which just segments sentences based on specific word clues, has similar performance in terms of readability. Also note that the use of readability formulas for assessing sentence simplicity is a controversial issue (see Chapter 2).

Table 5.1: Examples of original (CW), human simplified (SW), and machine simplified (TSM approach) sentences

CW	Genetic engineering has expanded the genes available to breeders to utilize in creating desired germ-lines for new crops.
SW	New plants were created with genetic engineering.
TSM	Engineering has expanded the genes available to breeders to use in making germ-lines for new crops.

5.3   OPTIMIZING RULE APPLICATION

Woodsend and Lapata's [2011] method has two main components. First, given a corpus of original and aligned simplified sentences which are both parsed, they learn simplification rules from this data. Then, given an input sentence, they generate all possible simplifications and choose the "best" simplification based on grammaticality constraints. In order to learn the simplification rules from the parsed data, they use a quasi-synchronous grammar which allows them to describe non-isomorphic parse tree pairs of the original and simplified versions.[1] Two types of rules are learned: lexical simplification rules and sentence splitting rules. A splitting rule will learn to separate the original sentence into a main sentence and an auxiliary sentence. Rules may include the addition of linguistic information such as a missing subject into the auxiliary sentence; this is actually done without considering context, thus allowing the production of nonsensical output. An optimization step based on Integer Linear Programming (ILP) [Schrijver, 1986] is proposed. They apply rules to the original sentence and if multiple rules match a given tree node, all alternatives are produced. The ILP model is in charge of selecting an optimal simplification by maximizing a cost function subject to a number of restrictions including readability constraints. Local restrictions control grammaticality of the output by ensuring that phrase dependencies are maintained, auxiliary sentences are included only if the main sentence is included, and that only one simplification alternative is chosen if more than one apply. By imposing readability constraints at the sentence level instead of at the text level, the model will aggressively try to split a sentence in order to obtain fewer words per sentence.

An inspection of the lexical rules learned from the corpus indicates that coverage of the approach is a real issue. The same can be said of the syntactic simplification rules. Any syntactic phenomenon which is known to cause difficulty but is not observed in the corpus is left untreated.

De Belder [2014] also applies ILP to the simplification of English sentences. He generates all possible simplifications for sentences using rules from Woodsend and Lapata [2011] and combines different solutions solving an ILP program where the objective function aims at minimizing the difference between the grade level of the simplified text and the expected grade level.

---

[1]For example, consider semantically equivalent non-isomorphic (syntactically) phrases such as "The boy kissed the girl" and "The boy gave a kiss to the girl" [Eisner, 2003].

His modeling is not without problems since his formulation became a quadratic programming problem which is not as easy to solve. Isolating the constraints of the readability formula into independent constraints led to a pure ILP problem which could be attempted. Each sentence has a penalty based on the rules that generated it, each of which has a penalty value obtained as the frequency in a corpus divided by the sum of the frequencies of all rules that could have been applied to the original sentence. A salience model is trained using Literacy Works (see Section 1.2) to identify which sentences should be kept in the simplified version of a text. The objective function to optimize is the sum of coefficients for grammaticality penalty and salience.

In a similar approach, manually developed rules combined with an optimization procedure are applied to the simplification of French sentences (Brouwers et al. [2014]). In order to develop rules, a corpus study is carried out to identify/typify simplification operations. 72 sentences from the French version of Wikipedia were aligned to 80 sentences from Vikidia, an encyclopedia for young people. Additionally, classic French narrative texts in original and simplified version were analyzed producing a set of 83 sentences aligned to 92 simpler (adapted) versions. Operations at the lexical, discourse, and syntactic level were observed. At the lexical level they observe synonym or hyperonym substitution, rewriting of anaphoric expressions, translation of foreign terms, etc. At the discourse level, reordering of information, deletion, personalization, etc. are identified. Acknowledging the fact that many operations are hardly implementable, they produce a set of 19 rules for deletion, modification (moving adverbials, "activisation," etc.), and splitting, which they apply recursively to the input sentence over-generating simplifications. The best simplification is selected using a Linear Integer Programming approach [Schrijver, 1986]. The ILP framework is instantiated via the contribution of four values of the text: (i) sentence length, (ii) mean word length, (iii) vocabulary familiarity, and (iv) presence of text keywords. A quantitative evaluation shows that, in the informative texts (encyclopedic articles) most errors (almost 90%) can be attributed to the text preprocessing stages, while in the narrative corpus the pre-processing is responsible for just over 50% of the errors. Most simplification errors, which can be attributed to few rules, arise because of incorrect removal of non-removable subordinates, which are difficult to distinguish automatically.

Klerke and Søgaard [2013] also rely on an over-generation approach to syntactic simplification in Danish. They use a dependency parsed corpus of original texts and random deletion of parts of the sentence. Sentence splitting is performed at relative clauses, coordinations, and conjunctions making sure that split components contain at least three words including at least one noun and one verb. The split sentences can be randomly deleted to produce simpler output. Structural heuristics can also be imposed so that split sentences containing subject, object, and negations are blocked. Simplifications are produced for each sentence by randomly removing components, these generated simplifications are scored considering three features: sentence readability—using the Lix readability index [Anderson, 1981], perplexity, and word-class distribution (variation in POS tag assignment when compared to distribution in a corpus). A baseline system is a MT-based simplifier where phrase translations are learned from an aligned original-simplified corpus and the language model is learned from a non-aligned big corpus. Evaluation considers appropriateness for beginner readers and grammaticality. A combined system (split, heuristics, selection) makes radical changes and is close to human simplification in terms of appropriateness, whereas the baseline MT approach is very conservative—as already acknowledged in most previous works.

5.4   LEARNING FROM A SEMANTIC REPRESENTATION

Narayan and Gardent [2014] add semantics into the simplification problem. They argue that approaches such as those of Woodsend and Lapata [2011] or Zhu et al. [2010] fail because they only consider syntactic information in the rule-induction process. As a consequence, phenomena such as choice of pronoun, which are important in generating sentences out of relative clauses, are not properly tackled because of lack of semantic information.

They also argue quite naturally that the current MT-based approaches to simplification fail to model syntactic transformations. Therefore their proposal combines a specialized semantic model that deals with split and delete operations with a translation-based model in charge of word substitution and reordering.

The authors also argue that both sentence splitting and phrase deletion are semantic in nature in the sense that split operations can be applied when an entity participates in two distinct events expressed in a sentence and that a deletion model should know about obligatory and optional event arguments.

In order to represent textual content semantically, they rely on Kamp's Discourse Representation Structure (DRS) [Kamp, 1981], which they compute automatically for each text using Boxer [Curran et al., 2007]. The semantic representation obtained is a graph representing connections between variables in the DRS. Probabilistic splitting is modeled using only thematic roles associated to event variables. Probabilities for deletion are computed for prepositional phrases, adjectives and adverbs, and orphan words (i.e., words which become unconnected after a split operation). For prepositional phrases, features are the preposition and the PP-length range while for orphan words the features are the orphan word and whether the word is at a boundary of the representation.

The full model can be interpreted as the application of the following steps: (i) a semantic model for splits and deletion (DRS-SM), (ii) a phrase-based mono-lingual translation model for word replacement and word order, and (iii) a probabilistic language model. Training of the DRS-SM model is done following the approach suggested by Zhu et al. where the training data (aligned EW/SEW sentences) is automatically created by iterative application of split and delete operations to the initial representation. Parameter estimation is done using the EM algorithm [Dempster et al., 1977].

Evaluation compares the output of their system with other three approaches: Zhu et al. [2010], Woodsend and Lapata [2011], and Wubben et al. [2012]. BLEU is used to compare the systems' output against gold simplifications. The Levenshtein distance (see Navarro [2001] for example) between automatic simplification and the original and gold simplification and the number of automatic simplifications identical to the original and the gold are also computed. In all metrics the semantic-based approach is better: they obtain a higher BLEU score, more simplifications identical to the gold (3%), and few sentences identical to the original sentence. Human assessment for simplicity, fluency and adequacy is also carried out, obtaining rather positive results.

5.5   CONCLUSION

In recent years, the use of machine learning in various subfields of computational linguistics has intensified. Text simplification is not immune to this trend. The availability of corpora of original and simplified sentences is key to learn syntactic and lexical transformations. However, available text simplification datasets are scarce or not fit for the learning task because they are either too simplistic or too complex. Many text simplification approaches use a statistical machine translation paradigm which, when trained in simplistic datasets, produce simplifications almost identical to the input text or sentence. Recent work has shown that semantic information is important to achieve better results. Since producing huge simplification datasets is unlikely to occur, future methods should pay more attention to unsupervised or semi-supervised techniques which are able to learn from a handful of examples together with huge amounts of non-simplified material.

5.6   FURTHER READING

Related to the problem of learning simplification operations is the use of machine learning to assess whether sentences should be simplified. Since readability assessment at sentence level is still an under-developed subject, researchers have come up with classification systems to decide, for example, whether sentences should be reduced, split, or deleted. Examples of these approaches are covered by Petersen and Ostendorf [2007], Štajner and Saggion [2013b] and Gasperin et al. [2009b] each addressing a different language. Also, given pairs of original and simplified sentences, some researchers have proposed procedures to classify the type of operations involved in the transformation: Medero and Ostendorf [2011] identify splits, omissions, and expansions while Amancio and Specia [2014] identify splits, insertions, reordering, and paraphase.

CHAPTER 6

Full Text Simplification Systems

More than ten years ago, the idea of creating a simplification system (PSET) for a specific target population, people suffering from aphasia, emerged. Following that seminal work, in recent years a number of proposals have been attempted to create full systems able to produce simplified output automatically. This chapter looks in some detail at three systems for different readerships and languages: PSET for English, Simplext for Spanish, and PorSimples for Brazilian Portuguese. These systems have been chosen because they have been designed for specific target populations (people with aphasia, people with low literacy, and people with cognitive disabilities) and they have been thoroughly described in several relevant research papers. Furthermore, unlike other existing approaches, some of these systems resulted in useful applications which have been tested with the target users.

6.1 TEXT SIMPLIFICATION IN PSET

Probably one of the best-known full simplification systems has been developed in the Practical Simplification of English Texts (PSET) project [Canning et al., 2000, Carroll et al., 1998, Devlin and Tait, 1998], a UK initiative to produce adapted texts for aphasic people. In addition to peer-reviewed literature on aphasia and readability, Devlin and Tait [1998] carried out field work to identify what type of simplification may benefit people with aphasia. They arrived at the conclusion that aphasic readers may be more likely to comprehend sentences which are simpler that those which are complex. They proposed that sentences should:

- follow the simple subject-verb-object (SVO) pattern;

- be in active voice;

- be as short as possible, containing only one clause and one base preposition;

- contain only one adjective per noun;

- be chronological in that the order of the sentences in the text reflects the order of the events described; and

- be semantically non-reversible (e.g., aphasic readers may find it difficult to correctly interpret passive constructions).

The authors also examined the peculiarities of newspaper discourse, which is beyond the full comprehension of many aphasic readers. Some characteristics of newspaper articles which make them difficult to comprehend are: long sentences, overuse of compound nouns and adjectives (e.g., "Twenty-five-year-old blonde-haired mother-of-two Jane Smith..."), position of the adverbials in the sentences, etc.

The implemented PSET system was composed of three main components: a syntactic simplifier, an anaphora resolver and substitution component, and a lexical simplifier. The input texts were processed with a probabilistic parser. The syntactic simplifier, SYSTAR [Briscoe and Carroll, 1995], used rules to match "simplifiable" text patterns which are used to change the sentence according to specific transformations. Rules are recursively applied until no pattern unification occurs. The system was able to deal with agentive passives and compound sentences. During rule application the system ensures that the NP matching the by-agent in the passive construction can function as subject of the active sentence. Seven types of passive verb clauses are dealt with by SYSTAR. During testing, all compound sentences were correctly split while about seventy percent of all passives which were transformed were actually acceptable. A pronoun resolution algorithm was included with the aim of replacing pronouns with their antecedent noun phrases, having recognized pronouns as specially difficult linguistic phenomenon for aphasic readers. Lexical simplification in PSET was implemented as a synonym replacement procedure where a difficult word was replaced—without word sense disambiguation—with its more-frequent synonym found in WordNet (see Section 3.1). The work was continued later on in the HAPPI project [Devlin and Unthank, 2006] to develop a web-based interface for people to simplify texts online.

6.2   TEXT SIMPLIFICATION IN SIMPLEXT

Simplext [Saggion et al., 2015b] aimed at developing simplification technology for Spanish speakers with intellectual disabilities (ID). The simplification solution had an educational and social function, since it targeted people with ID who undertake training in university programs designed for insertion in the marketplace. In order to have data for the study of simplification phenomena and since no available corpus of original and adapted texts exists for Spanish, a specially designed corpus was created. It contains original news articles from a Spanish news agency and their adaptations which were carefully produced by trained experts, and are based on specific guidelines produced for the project. Since the editing process itself was not recorded, a program was specially designed to align the text at sentence level [Bott and Saggion, 2011a]. The automatic alignment was then hand-corrected with a graphical editing tool available in the GATE framework [Maynard et al., 2002]. Sentence alignment is crucial for corpus studies and also for possible machine learning experiments which might be conducted on specific sub-problems of text simplification. Examples of original sentences and their manual simplifications are shown in Table 6.1. The examples illustrate typical transformations in the corpus.

- Example 1 shows an instance of simplification of the vocabulary. The word *sucursal* (branch) in the original sentence is replaced by its synonym *oficina* (office) (10 times more frequent

Table 6.1: Fragments of the Simplext corpus (original and simplified sentence pairs)

Example	Original	Simplified
1	*Abre en Madrid su primera* **sucursal** *el mayor banco de China y del Mundo.* (Opens in Madrid its first branch the biggest bank of China and the World.)	*El banco mas importante de China y del mundo abre una* **oficina** *en Madrid.* (The most important bank of China and the world opens an office in Madrid.)
2	*El ICBC ha abierto ya 203* **sucursales** *en un total de 28 países de todo el mudo, también en España desde este lunes.* (The ICBC has opened 203 branches in a total of 28 countries around the world, also in Spain since this Monday.)	*El Banco de China tiene* **oficinas** *en muchos países del mundo. Ahora, tabién tiene una oficina en España.* (The Bank of China has offices in many countries around the world. Now it also has an office in Spain.)
3	*Como muestra de su envergadura, según datos de 2009, el ICBC tenía en nómina a un total de 386.723 empleados, sólo en China, en un total de 16.232 sucursales.* (As a sign of its size and according to data from 2009, the ICBC had a total of 386,723 employees in China only, in 16,232 branches.)	
4	**Arranca** *la liga masculina de Goalball, el único deporte específico para ciegos.* (Starts the men's league of Goalball, the only specific sport for the blind.)	**Comienza** *la liga masculina de Goalball. El Goalball es el único deporte específico para ciegos.* (Begins the men's league of Goalball. Goalball is the only specific sport for the blind.)
5	*La ONU prevé el fin de muertos por malaria para 2015.* (The UN expects the end of deaths by malaria for 2015.)	*La ONU cree que ninguna persona moriria por malariá a partir de 2015. La ONU es la Organización de las Naciones Unidas. La malaria es ua enfermedad que se transmite gracias a un mosquito.* (The UN believes that nobody will die of malaria from 2015. The UN is the United Nations Organization. Malaria is a disease transmited by a mosquito.)

according to the Spanish Royal Academy's frequency list)[1] in the simplification. It also shows a syntactic transformation in order to have a simplified sentence with the Subject Verb Object (SVO) syntactic pattern, which is the natural order of syntactic elements in a sentence in Spanish.

- Example 2, in addition to the replacement of *sucursal* by *oficina*, shows an interesting case of summarization of detailed information: the replacement of *en 28 países del mundo* (in 28 countries around the world) by *en muchos países del mundo* (in many countries around the world). The example also presents a splitting operation.

- Example 3 exemplifies a delete operation by which a full sentence is not included in the simplified text. This is a frequent operation in the Simplext corpus that occurs in over 70% of simplified documents [Štajner et al., 2013].

- Example 4 shows a splitting operation together with the replacement of the verb *arranca* (starts) by its more common synonym *comienza* (begins) (seven times more frequent according to the Spanish Royal Academy's frequency list).[1]

- Example 5 is a case of clarification, where the human editor includes "definitions" of "difficult" terms such as the abbreviation *ONU* and the term *malaria*.

In addition to these more or less standard simplifications, strong re-writting cases were observed such the example below.

Original: *Amnistía Internacional acusó a las autoridades estadounidenses de proporcionar un "trato inhumano" a Bradley Manning, un soldado acusado de filtrar "cables" de la diplomacia norteamericana al portal Wikileaks.* (Amnesty International accused the U.S. authorities to provide an "inhuman" treatment to Bradley Manning, a soldier accused of leaking "wires" of American diplomacy to the website Wikileaks.)

Simplification: *Estados Unidos trata muy mal a un soldado detenido. El soldado se llama Bradley Manning. Bradley Manning está detenido por dar información del gobierno de Estados Unidos a Wikileaks. Wikileaks es una página web donde se da información sobre asuntos de interés público.* (United States treats very bad a soldier in prison. The soldier is called Bradley Manning. Bradley Manning is in prison for giving information about the Government of the United States to Wikileaks. Wikileaks is a website which provides information on matters of public interest.)

Bott and Saggion [2011b] carried out an analysis of the corpus in order to qualify and quantify simplification operations and decide on their eventual computational implementation. The Simplext corpus has been used for simplification decisions [Drndarević and Saggion, 2012b]

---

[1]Real Academia Española: Database (CREA) [online]. Corpus de referencia del español actual. http://www.rae.es

and machine translation experiments [Štajner, 2014]. The Simplext system consists of three modules: a rule-based lexical simplification component, a synonym-based simplification component, which uses a thesaurus and distance measures from distributional semantics, and a syntactic simplification grammar. The choice and the design of the modules was based on the two corpus studies. The lexical simplification component has been described in Section 3.2.

6.2.1 RULE-BASED "LEXICAL" SIMPLIFICATION

The second component of Simplext is a lexical simplification algorithm based on synonym substitution; we do not describe it here since the method has been already presented in Section 3.2. The third component of the Simplext system performs additional simplifications which cannot be dealt with by a synonyms dictionary but need a rule-based approach. Based on a corpus study [Drndarević and Saggion, 2012a, Drndarević et al., 2013] (see Section 1.1), a set of re-writing rules were implemented, including the normalization of reporting verbs, the reduction of sentence content, some clarification, and the normalization or reduction of numerical information content. A rule was implemented to eliminate all parenthetical information from the sentences. A set of rules was implemented to normalize reporting verbs which are ubiquitous in newspaper articles. It was observed that different reporting verbs in the 40 original texts of the Simplext corpus such as *warn*, *confirm*, *assure*, *suggest*, *say*, *explain*, *inform*, etc. were all transformed at least once into the verb *decir* (*say*), which is simpler and less ambiguous than any of the other verbs. The rules looking into the context of the reporting verb were implemented to ensure that the substitution is valid (e.g., substitution with the verb *say* leaves the syntactic structure correct). The original list of reporting verbs from the corpus was expanded using a thesaurus to obtain 32 different verbs in order to have a good coverage on unseen documents (see Drndarević et al. [2012] for details). The decision of substituting all reporting verbs was justified by the fact that *decir* is both the most common and the most general reporting verb [Bosque Muñoz and Demonte Barreto, 1999, Quirk et al., 1985] and shorter than any of its semantic equivalents, which complies with the rules present in the "Make it Simple" guidelines [Freyhoff et al., 1998]. The authors also found that substitution of any reporting verb with *decir* eliminates polysemy, as is the case with the verb *indicar*, which in Spanish means both "point" (the literal meaning) and "point out" (non-literal meaning). As stated in the WCAG 2.0 guidelines [W3C, 2008], the use of non-literal meaning should be avoided in easy-to-read writing.

Where numerical expressions are concerned, the most common simplification operation is that numerical expressions are usually eliminated, probably because they convey too detailed information which could be dropped without harming the essential message. Other simplification operations frequent enough to justify their implementation were the transformation of numbers in words into their equivalent numerical expressions (for numbers in the range from 1–10), the addition of the word "year" to the numerical representation of years (e.g., "year 1999" instead of "1999"), the transformation of named periods (e.g., decades, centuries) into their corresponding meaning (e.g., "20 years" instead of "two decades"), and the reduction of dates comprising a year to the year itself (e.g., "by 2010" instead of "by the end of May 2010"). This latter operation requires accurate identification of a number of complex constructions for which 47 rules have been implemented and tested (note that these rules are different from those described in Section 3.7; in fact, in Simplext the treatment of numbers is rather limited). These simplification operations were implemented using the Java Annotation Pattern Engine from the GATE system [Cunningham et al., 2000]. The rules, which were manually designed, rely on lexical, part-of-speech tags, and dictionary information (e.g., reporting verbs, adjectives of nationality, keywords). An evaluation of the rules over a set of randomly selected unseen documents from the corpus revealed perfect precision although limited recall. For example, rules that transform reporting verbs achieved perfect precision and 0.74 recall, while rules that transform numerical information achieved perfect precision and 0.84 recall.

6.2.2   COMPUTATIONAL GRAMMARS FOR SIMPLIFICATION

The syntactic simplification component consists of a hand-written computational grammar and focuses on the reduction of structural complexity. Several types of sentence splitting operations are performed: subordinate and coordinate structures, such as relative clauses, gerund constructions and VP coordinations are split into separate sentences, producing shorter and syntactically less complex outputs. The syntactic simplification module operates on syntactic dependency trees where tree manipulation is modeled as graph transduction. The graph transduction rules are implemented in the MATE framework [Bohnet et al.], in which the rules are gathered in grammars that apply in a pipeline: a first grammar applies to an input sentence as shown in Figure 6.1, and then each grammar is applied to the output produced by the previous grammar. Eight grammars consisting of around 140 rules have been developed to deal with the lexical substitutions performed during lexical simplification, to perform the syntactic simplification, to clean the output and return a well-formed sentence.

First of all, the **lexical substitution grammars** control the syntactic agreements between the substitute words and the original words of the sentence. For instance, if a masculine noun is replaced by a feminine one, the system has to change the gender of the determiners, adjectives, etc. accordingly. Second, the **syntactic simplification grammars** modify the structure of the sentences. Five types of syntactic simplification take place:

- participial modifiers are separated from their governing noun to form a new sentence;

- non-defining relative clauses preceded by a comma or those modifying an indefinite noun are also separated to form a new sentence;

- quoted direct objects are systematically positioned *after* the speech verb that introduces the quote;

- sentences which contain coordinated main verbs are split (one sentence per verb); and

- sentences with long coordinated objects are split.

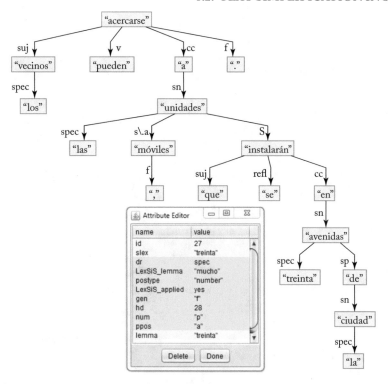

Figure 6.1: A syntactic input structure corresponding to sentence *Los vecinos pueden acercarse a las unidaded móviles, que se instalarán en treinta avenidas de la ciudad.* (The neighbors can approach the mobile units. These units will be installed on thirty avenues through the city.)

The syntactic simplification identifies all possible simplifications, chooses the simplifications to be performed, and finally applies the transformations.

Figure 6.2 shows the output of the second grammar for the structure of Figure 6.1. A chunk corresponding to the whole relative clause has been identified in which the relative pronoun *que* (that) contains all the necessary information (as attribute and values) for the modifications to take place: which rule has applied, the fact that the node label has to be changed, the name, gender, number of the antecedent, the fact that this node needs a deictic determiner, etc. The output of the third grammar when applied to the structure in Figure 6.2 is shown in Figure 6.3.

The grammars have been evaluated in terms of precision and recall, looking at correct rule applications in Bott et al. [2012b] and all the possible target constructions where the rules should have been applied. The evaluation was done for separate grammatical construction types. The precision was calculated as the ratio between correct applications and all applications of each rule, while recall was defined as the ratio between correct applications and the target constructions which should have been simplified. For the most frequent target constructions, which are rela-

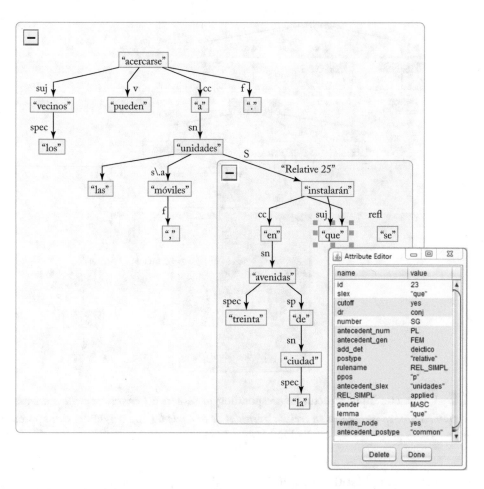

Figure 6.2: A sample of the output produced by the simplification grammar.

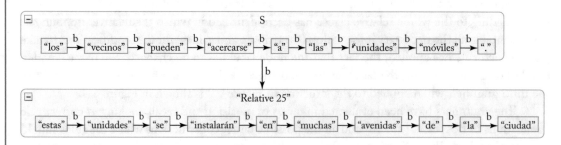

Figure 6.3: Sequence of tokens to be generated (the **b** label is used to represent precedence relations).

tive clauses and gerund constructions, precision/recall values are 0.39/0.66 (relative clauses) and 0.63/0.21 (gerunds). As for object coordination constructions, values were 0.42/0.58, reaching 0.65/0.50 for VP and clausal coordination.

6.2.3   EVALUATING SIMPLEXT

The Simplext system described above, that is the combination of the syntactic component with the rule-based system enriched with a module dedicated to numerical expression simplification [Bautista and Saggion, 2014], was evaluated on three dimensions: (i) the level of simplification achieved when compared with original and gold standard simplifications; (ii) the grammaticality of the output produced; and (iii) the preservation of the content of the original input. To measure the level of simplification achieved, readability formulas for Spanish were applied to 100 manually simplified (Manual) and 100 machine-simplified (Simplext) versions of 100 original texts (Original) from the Simplext corpus. The readability formulas used were three (see Chapter 2 for formulas details): the Spaulding Spanish readability (SSR) formula [Spaulding, 1956], the Sentence Complexity Index (SCI), and the Lexical Complexity Index (LCI) [Anula Rebollo, 2009]. The results of the experiment indicate significant differences in the average values of the formulas as well as significant pairwise differences between the different text types. According to the formulas, the manually simplified texts were easier than the machine-simplified, which were easier than the original texts. In order to assess grammaticality and meaning preservation, online questionnaires with 38 pairs of original and simplified sentences were prepared and administered to 25 Spanish informants. The items in the questionnaire contained an original sentence and its simplified version, where the simplified version had to contain at least one syntactic and one lexical simplification. The order of the sentences was alternated. Informants were asked to rate the grammaticality of each sentence and assess whether the two fragments conveyed the same meaning. Responses were given on a 5-point Likert scale with value 1 indicating strong disagreement and value 5 strong agreement. The grammaticality of the automatic simplified output was rated quite positively (scores 4 or 5) in 58% of the cases while preservation of meaning was rated positively in about 68% of the cases. The authors argue that almost one-third of syntactic simplification errors could be explained in terms of incorrect parsing. A number of errors were incorrect rule application for which rule re-engineering would be required. Lexical transformation errors were explained in terms of bad choice of modifiers to simplify numerical expressions ("another almost 30 houses"). Most meaning preservation problems were seen as dependent on ungrammaticality.

6.3   TEXT SIMPLIFICATION IN PORSIMPLES

The PorSimples project developed text simplification technology for the Brazilian Portuguese language [Aluísio and Gasperin, 2010, Gasperin et al., 2009b]. The motivation for such a project was to develop an automatic system and editing assistance tool to produce text adapted to the needs of people with low literacy, who, according to the authors, account for 11% of the Brazilian

Table 6.2: Fragments of the PortSimples corpus (original, natural, and strong simplifications)

Original	As salas de cinema de todo o mundo exibiam uma produção do diretor Joe Dante em que um cardume de piranhas escapava de um laboratório militar e atacava participantes de um festival aquático. (Movie theaters around the world exhibited a production of director Joe Dante where a school of piranhas escape from a military laboratory and attacked participants of an aquatic festival.)
Natural	As salas de cinema de todo o mundo exibiam uma produção do diretor Joe Dante. Em a produção do diretor Joe Dante, um cardume de piranhas escapava de um laboratório militar e atacava participantes de um festival aquático. (Movie theaters around the world exhibited a production of director Joe Dante. In production of director Joe Dante, a school of piranhas escape from a military laboratory and attacked participants of an aquatic festival.)
Strong	As salas de cinema de todo o mundo exibiam um lme do diretor Joe Dante. Em o lme, um cardume de piranhas escapava de um laboratório militar. O cardume de piranhas atacava participantes de um festival aquático. (Movie theaters around the world show a film of director Joe Dante. In the film, a school of piranhas escape from a military laboratory. The school of piranhas attacked participants of an aquatic festival.)

population.[2] A corpus of newspapers articles from a Brazilian newspaper called *Zero Hora* was created and simplified following two different simplification strategies. They were applied following a set of simplification guidelines targeting six different syntactic constructs worth simplifying: (1) appositions, (2) relative clases, (3) subordinate clauses, (4) coordinate clauses, (5) sentences with non-finite verbs, and (6) passive voice. First, a *natural* simplification strategy was applied in a parsimonious way to the sentences. In this strategy the human editor decided when to apply the simplification recommendations. From the natural simplified text, *strong* simplifications were produced. In this case, the guidelines were strictly applied in order to make sentences as simple as possible. While natural simplifications are intended for readers with basic literacy skills, strong simplifications target readers with rudimentary literacy skills. See Table 6.2 for an example of original and simplified sentences in PortSimples. The resulting parallel corpus contains 2,116 original sentences and 3,104 natural and 3,537 strong simplifications.

The operations considered in the automatic simplification system were:

1. non-simplification;

2. simple rewriting;

---

[2]Data from 2005.

3. strong rewriting;

4. convert into canonical subject-verb-object order;

5. convert from passive to active voice;

6. invert clause ordering;

7. splitting;

8. joining;

9. dropping sentence;

10. dropping sentence part; and

11. lexical substitution.

The two most productive operations observed in the corpus were lexical substitution (46%) followed by sentence splitting (34%). It is worth noting that although lexical substitutions are very frequent in the corpus, the authors' approach concentrates more on syntactic simplification and lexical simplification is mostly dealt with by a machine translation approach [Specia, 2010], explained in Section 5.1.

Where sentence splitting is concerned, a machine-learning approach is attempted in order to learn whether a sentence should be split [Gasperin et al., 2009a]. The approach, which combines a set of 26 basic features (sentence length, POS statistics, etc.) and 50 features based on rhetorical relations with a SVMs, achieves a 73.40 F-measure (see Section 1.1 for similar studies). Note that such a classifier would not perform the actual simplification, much less detecting the split point in a sentence. The actual simplification procedure is left to a set of hand-made developed procedures applied in cascade. The simplification procedure is recursive in that a simplification rule is applied and the resulting text re-parsed and eventually simplified again. The specific order in which rules are applied is: transformation of passive voice, treatment of oppositions, treatment of subordination, treatment of non-restrictive clauses, treatment of restrictive relatives, and treatment of coordinations. A preliminary evaluation of the rule-based system shows relatively good performance for sentence splitting operations, but poor performance for more complex transformations such as SVO re-ordering.

6.3.1   AN AUTHORING TOOL WITH SIMPLIFICATION CAPABILITIES

SIMPLIFICA [Aluísio et al., 2010], an authoring tool developed in the context of PosSimples, helps writers simplify texts until a certain readability grade level is achieved. The tool is able to propose to a writer simplifications which can then be corrected to ensure good text quality. The writer can assess the readability of the text according to three levels: rudimentary, basic, and advanced. The assessment is carried out by a text classification algorithm (a SVM from the

WEKA tool [Hall et al., 2009]), which uses a number of cognitive, structural, syntactic, and n-gram features. Cognitively motivated metrics are based on the Coh-Metrix tool [Graesser et al., 2004], which the authors adapted to Portuguese in the Coh-Metrix-PORT. In order to train the classifier, the PorSimples corpus is used after having been expanded with articles from other sources. The authors found that considering the three readability levels in an ordinal scale instead of as standard multi-class classification yields better results. Given the relatively good classification performance obtained (F-score 0.91 in cross-validation experiments), the classifier was included in SIMPLIFICA.

6.4   CONCLUSION

The objective of this chapter was to present a number of efforts to provide simplification technology to specific audiences in different languages: people with aphasia (English), people with low-literacy (Portuguese), and people with intellectual disabilities (Spanish). The PETS project was based on peer-reviewed literature and some field work so as to understand the simplification needs of people with aphasia. The PortSimples project aimed at people with low-literacy and its development was mainly based on a corpus of simplifications produced for the target audience. The Simplext system was developed based on corpus analysis and peer-reviewed literature. Since having target users available at different stages of system development is sometimes infeasible, alternative evaluation procedures were proposed by these projects in order to assess system components. Future systems should consider how to better model the user of the simplification, something most systems fall short of.

6.5   FURTHER READING

Several papers developed in the context of the *FIRST* project (to be covered in Chapter 7) have addressed different aspects of the simplification problem. For example, an overview of the project is covered by Martín-Valdivia et al. [2014] while simplification corpus development is covered in Štajner et al. [2014]. The *Able To Include* project, which is developing English and Spanish simplification for people with intellectual or developmental disabilities, was already described in Chapter 2. It also addresses access to textual content by means of pictographs using an computational linguistic approach which the reader may find interesting to read [Vandeghinste and Schuurman, Vandeghinste et al., 2015].

CHAPTER 7

Applications of Automatic Text Simplification

Over the past decade, automatic text simplification has been seen as an essential tool for improving the inclusion of people with special needs or to promote social inclusion. It has also continued to be seen as a natural language processing tool which can be used as a pre-processing step to help other natural language tasks. The chapter first presents an overview of approaches for specific target populations (not covered in Chapter 6) to then describe the use of text simplification technology to facilitate some tasks such as parsing, information extraction, or text summarization.

7.1 SIMPLIFICATION FOR SPECIFIC TARGET POPULATIONS

Pioneer work on adapting textual material to meet the needs of specific populations started with the PSET project already presented in Chapter 6. In recent years there has been a proliferation of projects investigating how to help reduce the complexity of texts according to the specific characteristics or problems faced by the target population. Applications have been produced for people with dyslexia, aphasia, deafness, ASD, etc. In the rest of this section, some of these approaches are presented.

7.1.1 AUTOMATIC TEXT SIMPLIFICATION FOR READING ASSISTANCE

Text simplification has been aimed at making texts more readable for congenitally deaf people, who tend to have difficulties in reading and writing [Inui et al., 2003]. Inui et al. focus on designing a computational model of the language proficiency of deaf people by collecting readability assessment data from teachers for the deaf. The data collected is a collection of pairs (s_i, s_j) of manually produced paraphrases indicating which element of the pair was likely to be easier to understand by the target population. Additionally, reasons for the judgments were recorded. Manually generated paraphrases were produced in a controlled way, removing from a sentence features, from a set of around fifty, that were the cause of difficulty in the original sentence. The collected dataset was used to train and test a readability ranking model to predict which (if either) of the elements of a given pair (s_i, s_j) of paraphrases was easier to read.

7.1.2   SIMPLIFICATION FOR DYSLEXIC READERS

Dyslexia is a specific learning disability with a neurological origin [Rello, 2014]. It is character-ized by difficulties with accurate and/or fluent word recognition and by poor spelling and decoding abilities. It is sometimes referred to as a specific reading disability while dysgraphia is a transcrip-tion disability. Where text simplification is concerned, it appears that tools which perform some sort of lexical "substitution" could help people with this learning disorder. Focusing on the Span-ish language, Rello et al. [2013b] studied the effect of word frequency and word length in read-ability (i.e., the easiness of reading) and comprehensibility (i.e., the easiness of comprehending) for people with dyslexia, finding that more frequent words increase readability for people with the dyslexia, while shorter words increase comprehensibility. Therefore, a tool which presents more frequent or shorter synonyms could be of help for people with dyslexia. In another study for Span-ish, Rello et al. [2013c] assessed the effect of numerical representation (in text) on readability and comprehensibility for people with dyslexia by analyzing the effect of digits vs. words (10 vs. ten), rounded vs. unrounded (almost 10 vs. 9.99), and percentages vs. fractions (25% versus 1/4). It was found that both digits (instead of words) and percentages (instead of fractions) improve readabil-ity for people with dyslexia; therefore a numerical simplification system could be of assistance for people with this disorder. However, Rello et al. [2013a] showed that directly replacing a word by a simpler synonym is subjectively not favored over a system that presents "simpler" synonyms on demand as a list.

7.1.3   SIMPLIFICATION-RELATED TECHNIQUES FOR PEOPLE WITH AUTISM SPECTRUM DISORDER

According to the *Oxford Dictionary of Psychology*, an autism spectrum disorder (ASD) "is a neu-rodevelopmental disorder characterized by gross and sustained impairment of social interaction and communication" [Colman, 2016]. People affected by the disorder experience delay or fail-ure of speech development, stereotyped and idiosyncratic language, or non-verbal behavior. In the context of the European FIRST project [Barbu et al., 2013, Martín-Valdivia et al., 2014], a multilingual tool (Bulgarian, English, and Spanish)—Open Book—to facilitate reading com-prehension for people with ASD was developed. Based on peer-reviewed literature and opin-ions from psychologists and careers of people with ASD, a number of language obstacles were identified including lexical obstacles (difficulty in understanding rare or specialized terms) and syntactic obstacles (for example, processing of relative clauses). Thirteen operations to remove language comprehension difficulties were identified. These include, for example, replacement of words by their simpler synonyms, splitting sentences to make them short, adding definitions of difficult terms, reducing the volume of the text by performing summarization, illustrating difficult concepts with retrieved images, or detecting and explaining figurative expressions. The syntactic simplification was carried out using a set of manually developed rules [Evans et al., 2014] mainly aimed at reducing sentences containing relative clauses. Additionally, figurative language detection relies on available dictionaries of idiom dictionaries with several lookup processes of various degrees of sophistication from exact match to pattern matching.

7.1.4   NATURAL LANGUAGE GENERATION FOR POOR READERS

From the natural language generation viewpoint, Williams and Reiter [2005] are interested in generating more readable texts for poor readers. They focus on a linguistic generation problem where a Rhetorical Structure Theory (RST) tree [Mann and Thompson, 1988] has to be transformed into a text which is easy to read by a target user. At the linguistic level, they are interested in generating texts which have simple and easy to understand words, short sentences, and simple syntactic structures. On the issue of discourse relation generation, they are interested in the choice of the cue phrase to express the relation, order of constituents in the relation, and use of punctuation between constituents. For example, they are interested in chosing the easiest sentence among the following possible equivalent sentences: "If you practise reading, your skills will improve," "If you practise reading, then your skills will improve," "Your skills will improve if you practise reading," etc. They created sets of hard constraint and optimization rules. Hard constraints are extracted from an annotated corpus of discourse relations in order to model correct cue phrase use. Two types of optimization rules are created. *Control rules* model the choice of common (more readable) cue phrases and penalization of ambiguous cue phrases. *Optimization rules* are based on enhanced-readability criteria drawn from psycholinguistic findings which indicate that discourse relations should be expressed by single cue phrases, more common cue phrases, and use of separate sentences for each relation component, etc. An evaluation of text produced using control and enhanced-readability criteria found that the enhanced-readability criteria produce more readable texts.

7.2   TEXT SIMPLIFICATION AS NLP FACILITATOR

The initial idea of Chandrasekar et al. [1996] was that sentences could be simplified in order to facilitate their processing by parsers which long ago were struggling with long and complicated constructions (see Section 4.1). Since that work, several researchers have resorted to text simplification to facilitate different natural language processing tasks or applications such as summarization or information extraction.

7.2.1   SIMPLIFICATION FOR PARSING

Jonnalagadda et al. [2009] argue that biomedical texts have a highly complex sentence structure posing important challenges for parsers trained on newspaper articles and that a simplification process, instead of parsing adaptation, might help dealing with such complexity. They use a two-step method to simplify sentences. First, rudimentary domain-specific text transformations are applied to the sentences where section indicators are removed from the sentences, names of genes are transformed into placeholders, and partially hyphenated words are completed in a context-aware fashion (e.g., "alpha-" is transformed into "alpha-catenin" in the context of "alpha- and beta-canetin"). The second step, which is based on parsing, involves the segmentation of the sentence into a sequence of clauses $c_1, c_2, ..., c_n$ using punctuation (commas) and iterative application of the parser to subsequences of clauses until a "correct" parse is produced (e.g., a parse containing a sentence link). The proposed approach improves the performance of the two parsers they tested their approach with in terms of average precision and recall of dependencies produced by the parser.

7.2.2 SIMPLIFICATION FOR INFORMATION EXTRACTION

Evans [2011], also in the biomedical domain, is interested in applying simplification techniques prior to extracting information from clinical vignettes which provide brief clinical descriptions of patients. Vignettes are structured in seven sections related to the patient visit: (1) basic information (gender, profession, etc.), (2) chief complaints (main patient concern), (3) history (family and medical history), (4) vital signs (pulse, blood pressure, etc.), (5) physical examination (clinical findings), (6) diagnostic study (results of the examination), and (7) laboratory study (laboratory results). Evans is particularly concerned with the simplification of coordinated and subordinated structures in the clinical descriptions such as: (i) "Examination shows jaundice, hypothermia, hypotonia, large anterior and posterior fontanels, and a hoarse cry" which may be difficult to deal with by rule-based information extraction. A simpler text to extract information from may be (2) "Examination shows a hoarse cry. Examination shows hypotonia. Examination shows large anterior fontanels. Examination shows large posterior fontanels. Examination shows..." which is a simplification of (1). While in (1) extraction rules will need to deal with complex coordination patterns, in (2) simple rules may suffice. Evans tested different classification algorithms based on conjunction (and, but, or, ",") and context to identify coordinations; further an iterative simplification algorithm is applied to create a single sentence from each conjoin. Evaluation is performed by comparing a system that uses complex information extraction patterns over coordinated structures with a system that extracts a single piece of information from a sentence. Results indicate that information extraction performance improves when simpler rules are applied over simplified input.

7.2.3 SIMPLIFICATION IN AND FOR TEXT SUMMARIZATION

Siddharthan et al. [2004] apply syntactic simplification of appositive and non-restrictive relative clauses before summarization. Their multi-document summarization algorithm contains four steps: (1) sentence simplification, (2) sentence clustering, (3) selection of relevant sentences from each cluster, and (4) generation of the final extractive summary. The authors argue that because the simplification operations remove the parenthetical from the main clause, the cluster quality is improved, therefore providing better clusters to pick sentences from. They also analyze sentence length and distribution of parenthetical clauses in human and machine summaries and found that considering those two variables, their summaries are closer to human summaries than automatic summaries produced by other systems.

Lal and Rüger [2002] are also interested in simplification for text summarization. However, and unlike the previous work, they are only interested in lexical simplification applied at the summary generation stage only. They use simple techniques similar to those of Carroll et al. [1998] (i.e., ranking synonyms using a psycholinguistic database) to replace difficult for more simple words. An evaluation of the summaries produced showed cases of wrong word replacement due to lack of word sense disambiguation or awkward use of words in context (e.g., "An aired event").

7.2.4   SIMPLIFYING MEDICAL LITERATURE

Ong et al. [2007] present an approach to simplify medical literature using (i) a dictionary of synonyms (for 53 medical terms) and definitions (for 415 terms), and (ii) a set of superficial transformation rules. Perhaps due to the nature of the documents, lexical simplification is blindly applied: if a word is found in the dictionary, then it is replaced by its simpler synonym in the dictionary or concatenated with its dictionary definition, creating an appositive construction. See example below:

> *People with weakened immune systems are more likely to get a brain abscess.*

> *People with weakened immune systems are more likely to get a brain abscess, a local accumulation of pus anywhere in the body.*

Syntactic simplification rules operate on the output of ANNIE, an information extraction system developed with the GATE system [Maynard et al., 2002], so they are rather superficial with respect to the amount of linguistic information they can use. As in Siddharthan [2006], they apply rules recursively, first tagging structures in the input sentence and then applying transformations according to what was found during analysis. See the following example.

> *Although fistula surgery is usually relatively straightforward, the potential for complication still exists.*

> *Fistula surgery is usually relatively straightforward. But the potential for complication still exists.*

7.2.5   RETRIEVING FACTS FROM SIMPLIFIED SENTENCES

Klebanov et al. [2004] propose the concept of "easy access sentence" (EAS) as a sentence from which it is easy to retrieve the information it contains. The operational definition of an EAS for a text T satisfies:

- EAS is grammatical;

- EAS has one finite verb;

- EAS does not make any claims not present in the text T; and

- the more named entities an EAS contains (instead of say pronouns or definite anaphora), the better.

To create EAS for a given text, the following "sentence simplification" procedure is applied to a text which has been processed by the Minipar parser [Lin, 2003]. For each verb V:

- if V is problematic (e.g., modal or belongs to an specific list of verbs) skip and continue with the next verb;

- if V is not finite, the tense is retrieved from the closest tensed governor verb;

- the dependents of the verb are collected from the dependencies produced by Minipar. The subject of the verb is retrieved, and in case no subject is found, the subject of the main clause the verb is attached to is set as subject;

- if any dependents are pronouns, they are replaced by their antecedents; and

- only structures which contain verbs and dependents are extracted.

Recall is evaluated using a gold standard created by 5 people for a 7-sentence text biography. 31 EASs produced by at least 3 people were considered as the final gold standard. Out of this set, 10 were produced by the automatic procedure (i.e., 30% recall).

7.2.6 SIMPLIFYING PATENT DOCUMENTS

Patents are legal documents with a very intricate and stereotypical structure [Burga et al., 2013, Ferraro, 2012]. This is particularly true for patent sentence claims characterized by their considerable length, complex syntactic structure with several embedded subordinate clauses and coordinations, and complicated multi-word terminology. See Table 7.1 for an example of a patent claim and how it can be made easier to read.

Bouayad-Agha et al. [2009] propose the simplification of patent claims in order to improve their comprehension and also to use simplified claims for summarization. Their approach segments claims into clauses, structures the clauses in a rhetorical tree (see Mann and Thompson [1988]) using weighted rules and a search algorithm, and then applies a rule-based reconstruction algorithm which completes NP clauses into full sentences. Examples of input and output can be seen in Table 7.1. The first item is a very long claim and the second is the simplification into more "readable" sentences.

7.3 CONCLUSION

This chapter provided an overview of the practical uses of automatic text simplification together with systems which have been developed to meet the needs of simplification in specific tasks: for systems, the need to reduce text complexity for easier post-processing; for humans, the need of simple texts to improve understanding of original complicated ones. Although in natural language

Table 7.1: A patent claim and its simplification

Original	Simplification
An automatic focusing device comprising: an objective lens for focusing a light beam emitted by a light source on a track of an information recording medium; a beam splitter for separating a reflected light beam reflected by the information recording medium at a focal spot thereon and through the objective lens from the light beam emitted by the light source; an astigmatic optical system including an optical element capable of causing the astigmatic aberration of the separated reflected light beam; a light detector having a light receiving surface divided, except the central portion thereof, into a plurality of light receiving sections which are arranged symmetrically with respect to a first axis extending in parallel to the axial direction of the optical element and to a second axis extending perpendicularly to the first axis and adapted to receive the reflected beam transmitted through the optical element and to give a light reception output signal corresponding to the shape of the spot of the reflected light beam formed on the light receiving surface;....	An automatic focusing device comprises: an objective lens; a beam splitter; an astigmatic optical system; a light detector; a focal position detecting circuit capable of giving an output signal and a lens driving circuit. The objective lens focusses light beam. The light source emits a light beam on a track of an information recording medium. The beam splitter separates the reflected light beam. The information recording medium reflects the reflected light beam at a focal spot thereon and through the objective lens from the light beam. The light source emits the light beam.

processing applications, such as parsing or information extraction, some works have reported improvement when text simplification technology is used as a preprocessing step, the picture is different for the direct use of simplified output by humans. In this sense, automatic text simplification for users is still in its infancy and much research is needed in order to provide better targeted solutions for real users.

7.4   FURTHER READING

Related to work in information extraction and similar to what we saw in Section 7.2.2, Wu et al. [2012] present the application of simplification to extract protein phosphorylation information, where it is shown that simplifying the text can increase by 20% the extraction of this specific information type. A further interesting application for simplification is question answering. As shown by Heilman and Smith [2010] and Bernhard et al. [2012], simple sentences can be quite effective for question generation. Where low-literacy readers are concerned, in addition to work by Gasperin et al. [2009a] on Portuguese, also worth examining is the work carried out in the context of the Educational Testing Service to develop tools to assess text difficulty and provide means for teachers to adapt textual material for non-native speakers [Burstein et al., 2013]. In a similar way and also for non-native students, Eskenazi et al. [2013] presents a study of the effect of automatic translation and manual simplification for making texts more accessible.

CHAPTER 8

Text Simplification Resources and Evaluation

Lexical resources and corpora are fundamental sources of knowledge for developing and testing simplification systems. This chapter focuses on lexical resources which contain, in addition to linguistic information, valuable psycholinguistic information which may contribute to the development of lexical simplification applications or the assessment of text readability. We also describe recent efforts aiming at the compilation of datasets which can be used as gold standards for lexical simplification evaluation. Where syntactic simplification is of concern, we describe the few comparable or parallel corpora which have been created and which developers can use to either develop or test their simplification solutions. Finally, we provide an account of evaluation efforts both in terms of metrics and methods in the area of text simplification research.

8.1 LEXICAL RESOURCES FOR SIMPLIFICATION APPLICATIONS

Gala et al. [2013] are interested in developing readability lexicons with degrees of difficulties for specific populations (in their case, people affected by Parkinson's disease). They have gathered a lexicon used by people affected by Parkinson's disease by extracting words from a corpus of spoken transcriptions from 20 patients affected by this disease. In order to grade each of the words extracted from the transcriptions, they relied on two databases: Manulex, a list of French words with observed frequencies from three different education levels textbooks, and JeuxDe-Mots, a crowd-sourced semantic network of words and associations (e.g., semantic or thematic relations). Manulex's words were given complexity scores based on the observed frequencies (i.e., a word was given the education level where it was first observed). JeuxDeMots contains words and associations collected through a serious game. For those words and synonyms absent from the resources, a machine learning approach was used to obtain word grades. A SVM algorithm (see Burges [1998] for example) was trained using a set of intra-lexical and psycholinguistic variables. Among the intra-lexical variables are word length, number of morphemes, word spelling patterns, etc. The psycholinguistic features include, for example, the number of the word's orthographic neighbors, lexical frequency, membership of a list of basic French words, etc. These variables were first assessed on their predictive power to discriminate the Parkinson vocabulary from a general vocabulary of the French language. The model was trained on all graded words from the

Manulex resource. Cross-validation experiments show 62% accuracy of the model, which leaves considerable space for improvement. Nevertheless, the model was applied to grade the words absent in Manulex to obtain a list of over 17,000 graded words.[1]

Brooke et al. [2012] present an approach to readability lexicon expansion. Starting from a manually created dataset of a *Difficulty* lexicon (of over 15,000 words) structured in three difficulty bands (beginner, intermediate, advanced), they try two approaches to evaluate lexicon expansion: (i) a regression model to associate a numerical score to words (0, 0.5, 1 depending on their difficulty) and (ii) a SVM to classify, given words w_1 and w_2, whether w_1 is more complex than w_2 or w_1 is easier than w_2. The novelty of the approach lies in the computation of some numerical features for words based on the texts where the word occurs. In order to model words in documents (from a corpus of over 1 million word types), reduced-dimension vector representations, computed with latent semantic analysis [Landauer and Dumais, 1997], are used. Given a word, features are computed as differences of cosine averages between the word in question and elements of two sets of seed words where each set represents opposite dimensions (e.g., formal–informal). In order to evaluate the performance of the system decisions on test data, they compute accuracy with respect to the Difficulty lexicon as well as accuracy with respect to crowd-sourced assessments from a word pairwise comparison task (i.e., comparing words with different *a priori* difficulties: beginner-intermediate, intermediate-advanced, beginner-advanced) where workers have to indicate the relative difference in difficulty between words. Results are over 87% accurate when compared with the Difficulty lexicon.

8.2 LEXICAL SIMPLIFICATION RESOURCES

Paetzold and Specia [2015] developed a Python library, LEXenstein, for evaluation of lexical simplification systems based on the availability of evaluation data. The authors consider lexical simplification to be composed of three tasks: (i) substitution generation, the task of gathering candidate word substitutions for complex words (out of context); (ii) substitution selection, the task of filtering word substitutions according to the context; and (iii) substitution ranking, the task of sorting the substitutions according to their simplicity (note that in Paetzold [2016] an additional step is considered). It is worth mentioning that there are a number of assumptions about the lexical substitution task in this work which are not always met by all approaches. For example, the gold standard contains substitutions ranked by simplicity. The metrics used for substitution generation and substitution selection are as follows.

- **Potential:** the proportion of cases in which the system proposed at least one substitution which is present in the gold standard.

- **Precision:** the ratio of proposed substitutions which are present in the gold standard to the total of proposed substitutions proposed.

- **F-measure:** the harmonic mean of Potential and Precision.

---

[1]http://resyf.lif.univ-mrs.fr/ResyfApplication/index.html

The metrics for evaluating substitution ranking are TRank@i and Recall@i (with $i = 1, 2, 3$). TRank@i, for example, is the proportion of cases in which the substitution candidates at rank i and above have non-empty intersection with the gold standard while Recall@i is the recall that the set of substitution candidates at ranks r ($r \leq i$) produce.

De Belder and Moens [2012] also made available a lexical simplification dataset created from the SemEval Lexical Substitution task (see Section 3.6). From the original dataset, the authors removed all target words which were listed in a list of *easy words*, which is the union of words in the Dale-Chall list of easy words (see Chapter 2) and the basic English word list from SimpleWikipedia. After removal, there remained 43 words and 430 sentences in the dataset. The dataset was annotated by Mechanical Turks and students, where the annotation task consisted of, given a sentence, a target word in the sentence, and a set of synonyms, ranking the different alternatives (i.e., synonyms plus target word) according to their simplicity (with ties allowed). The multiple annotations from the annotators were converted into a single gold-standard ranking. Figure 8.1 shows examples of the dataset while Figure 8.2 shows the final gold-standard rankings for each data-point. For evaluation of a lexical simplification system, De Belder and Moens [2012] propose the following metrics. In a *binary* evaluation metric, they consider that any substitution easier than the original will be valid. This is exemplified in case 987 with target word *liberal*, for example: suppose a system proposes as substitute the word *tolerant*, such a system will obtain one point since in this case the substitute is easier than the target. In a *rank evaluation*, the rank produced by the system is compared to the gold rank. Also specifically adapted precision and recall metrics are proposed.

Horn et al. [2014] present a lexical simplification method and dataset for evaluation of lexical simplification systems. The lexical simplifier learns simplification rules from aligned sentences from comparable pairs of documents. The dataset used was Coster and Kauchak's [2011] dataset from EW and SEW. The system first learns a set of rules of the form $w \rightarrow c_1, c_2, \ldots, c_n$ where c_i are candidate words. The rules are then filtered by excluding stop words, pairs of words without the same part of speech tag, and any word which has been labeled as a proper noun. Morphological variants are also added to the rules so as to account for unobserved replacements (e.g., if *automobile* $\rightarrow$ *car* is a valid rule, then also *automobiles* $\rightarrow$ *cars*). Given the multiple substitutions available for a given word, the authors cast lexical simplification as ranking; they use a SVM algorithm [Joachims, 2006] to learn a ranking function. Features to train the ranker are: (i) candidate probability: the proportion of times the candidate was used as replacement for the target word; (ii) frequency of the candidate from different corpora; and (iii) probabilities from four different language models, and (iv) two context frequencies (one or two words context window) for the candidate in the place of the target word as occurring in the Google n-grams corpus [Brants and Franz, 2006]. The generated dataset of lexical simplifications comprises 500 examples composed of a sentence and a target word, randomly sampled from alignments between sentences in EW and SEW, with assessments produced using Amazon's Mechanical Turk.[2] Fifty people

---

[2]https://www.mturk.com

1161	acquire.v	Thus, the analyst **acquires** knowledge about the nature of the patient through an awareness of something going on in him.
1165	acquire.v	How many times have I caught up with those people several years later, to discover that they have **acquired** a lifestyle, a car and a mortgage to match their salary, and that their initial ideals have faded to the haziest of memories, which they now dismiss as a post-adolescent fantasy?
986	liberal.a	Municipal housing schemes with **liberal** aid from the central government will be encouraged for those who do not wish to establish their own houses.
987	liberal.a	We're both in our early thirties, both grew up in the suburbs of east coast US cities, raised by **liberal** parents who pushed us towards soccer, the progressive, globalized, nonviolent sport of choice for seventies and eighties US parents.
1575	scene.n	Every **scene** seems totally natural like it could have really happened, and yet the movie is not a dull slice-of-life diorama either.
1577	scene.n	On the plus side, the immediate mode offers the possibility of exploring dynamic **scenes**.

Figure 8.1: Target words and sentences from De Belder and Moens's [2012] lexical simplification dataset.

1161	acquire.v	[[gain, gather, collect], [acquire], [amass]]
1165	acquire.v	[[get], [obtain, achieve, gain], [acquire, procure]]
986	liberal.a	[[generous], [abundant, plentiful, liberal, social]]
987	liberal.a	[[open minded, free thinking], [broad minded], [tolerant], [progressive, liberal]]
1575	scene.n	[[part, act], [setting, scene], [sequence]]
1577	scene.n	[[picture, area], [scene, setting], [sight], [sequence]]

Figure 8.2: Gold-standard replacements from De Belder and Moens's [2012] dataset for the example in Figure 8.1.

provided simplifications (i.e., lexical substitutes) for each sentence in the dataset. Counts for the lexical substitutes proposed were obtained so as to produce a frequency-based rank for the set of replacement.

Evaluation metrics in this work are: (i) precision: the percentage of system suggestions that appear in the human annotation, (ii) precision@k: the percentage of system suggestions appearing among the top k human annotations (as ranked by their counts in the human responses), (iii) accuracy: the percentage of cases (out of the total number of sentences) where the system proposed a change identical to one of the human annotations, and (iv) changed: the proportion of changes the system made.

occurrences	A haunted house is dened as a house that is believed to be a center for supernatural **occurrences** or paranormal phenomena.	events (24); happenings (12); activities (2); things (2); accidents (1); activity (1); acts (1); beings (1); event (1); happening (1); instances (1); times (1); situations (1)
acquired	Dodd simply retained his athletic director position, which he had **acquired** in 1950.	gotten (13); gained (11); got (7); received (7); obtained (5); achieved (3); amassed (1); inherited (1); taken (1); started (1)

Figure 8.3: Gold-standard lexical simplification dataset from Horn et al. [2014]. The first column contains the target simplification word. The second column contains a sentence where we have highlighted the target word. The third column shows the simpler substitutions provided by annotators together with their counts.

CASSA [Baeza-Yates et al., 2015] is a resource to perform lexical simplification in Spanish. It was created by combining two different resources: (i) the Spanish Open Thesausus (SOT)—already used in Spanish lexical simplification (see Section 3.2) and (ii) the 5-g Google Books Ngram Corpus [Lin et al., 2012]. In the resource, each 5-gram w_1, w_2, t, w_3, w_4 represents a target word t and its left (w_1, w_2) and right (w_3, w_4) context. In addition to the 5-gram there also is a list of possible substitutes for the target word, extracted from the senses listed in SOT which have also been observed in the context $w_1, w_2, ?, w_3, w_4$. These substitutes are sorted by frequency so that the most frequent can be used as a replacement of the target. Table 8.1 shows fragments of the resource: for example the first entry in the figure indicates the target word *ámbitos* (areas) which occurs in the context *todos los ámbitos de la* (all the areas of the). The possible substitutes of this target word in context are: *campo* (field), *ambiente* (environment), and *terreno* (field).

8.3   CORPORA

One of the most widely used datasets for trainable text simplification systems in English is the PWPK parallel complex-simple dataset compiled by Zhu et al. [2010]. They collected 65,133 ar-

Table 8.1: Fragment of the CASSA resource showing the target frequency, the target, the context of the target, the list of substitutes, and the target's lemma

Frequency	Target	Context $(w_1, w_2, ?, w_3, w_4)$	Substitutes	Lemma
60285	ámbitos	todos los ? de la	[campo, ambiente, terreno]	ámbito
59886	ocurre	lo que ? es que	[pasar, suceder, acontecer]	ocurrir
58326	tercio	el primer ? del siglo	[doblar, desplazar, inclinar]	terciar
58026	facultades	de las ? que le	[poder, licencia, autorización]	facultad
57511	mitad	a la ? de la	[parte, fracción, porcion]	mitad

ticles from Simple Wikipedia and Wikipedia paired by following the language link provided in the dump files in Wikimedia.[3] The JWPL[4] tool was used to extract the plain text of the articles, after which the texts were analyzed using the Stanford Parser [Klein and Manning, 2003] and the lemmatization program provided by Tree Tagger [Schmid, 1994]. The sentences in each pair of documents were aligned using an algorithm based on a term frequency and inverse document frequency combination, which was the best performing algorithm according to the authors. Table 8.2 features examples of aligned sentences in the PWPK dataset. Examples like (1) or (3) will be over-represented in this dataset. Also note that in (5) the simple sentence contains information which may contradict that in the complex sentence (three months vs. six months). Also in the simple sentence example (6) the information "the only means of transport there" is not present in the complex sentence.

The final dataset obtained contained over 108,000 sentence pairs. The average sentence lengths (in tokens) are: 25.01 for complex sentences and 20.87 for simple sentences. As already shown in Chapter 5, however, the suitability of the dataset for text simplification has been questioned many times (see Štajner et al. [2015]).

Although of reduced size and narrow content, the parallel corpus created by Barzilay and Elhadad [2003] from *Encyclopedia Britannica* and their manually adapted version for children is cited many times in text simplification research. Examples of the dataset are shown in Table 8.3.

Xu et al. [2015] heavily criticize the use of the Wikipedia dataset for research in text simplification. After analyzing a sample of aligned pairs in the PWKP dataset, they convincingly present problems with the dataset including the presence of alignment errors (an estimated 17% of pairs are not aligments), presence of inadequate simplifications (about 33% of the alignments contain no simpler element), and difficulty of generalizing well to other genres. These problems are inherent in the way in which simple Wikipedia was created, not as a parallel corpus, but as the result of spontaneous writing. There is therefore no "direct" relation, from the text adaptation

---

[3]http://download.wikimedia.org
[4]https://www.ukp.tu-darmstadt.de/software/jwpl/

Table 8.2: Examples of comparable text fragments from Wikipedia and Simple Wikipedia

Example	English Wikipedia	Simple English Wikipedia
1	April is the fourth month of the year in the Gregorian Calendar, and one of four months with a length of 30 days.	April is the fourth month of the year with 30 days.
2	This month was originally named Sextilis in Latin, because it was the sixth month in the ancient Roman calendar, which started in March about 735 BC under Romulus.	This month was first called Sextilis in Latin, because it was the sixth month in the old Roman calendar. The Roman calendar began in March about 735 BC with Romulus.
3	Dombasle-sur-Meurthe is a commune in the Meurthe-et-Moselle department in northeastern France.	Dombasle-sur-Meurthe is a town in France.
4	Konkani is the official language in the Indian state of Goa and is also one of the official languages of India.	It is the official language of Goa, a state in India.
5	The male fertilizes the eggs externally by releasing his sperm onto them, and will then guard them for at least three months, until they hatch.	After the fertilization of the eggs, the male will guard them for at least six months.
6	Transport Marske is served by Longbeck and Marske railway stations, which connect to Darlington mainline station.	The Longbeck railway station and Marske railway station, which connect to Darlington mainline station, are the only means of transport there.

viewpoint, between a Wikipedia article and a Simple Wikipedia article. The authors also observed that about 50% of the sentence pairs in the PWKP corpus are not simplifications.

The Newsela dataset is a more quality-controlled text simplification dataset which has been created with text simplification and adaptation in mind. It is a corpus of news articles re-written by professional editors to meet the readability standards for children at multiple grade levels. The corpus contains 1,130 news articles, each of them re-written 4 times for children at different grade levels, obtaining four simplification versions (simp-1 is the least simple and simp-4 the simpler; see Table 8.4 for different versions of an original news piece in Newsela). Newsela can be used to help teachers select material that matches the expertise of pupils. The original documents and simplifications were automatically aligned with a jaccard-similarity sentence alignment al-

Table 8.3: Examples of comparable text fragments from *Britannica* (adult and children versions)

Original	The Bernardino Rivadavia Argentine Museum of Natural Sciences has an exceptionally rich fossil collection and operates a scientific institute.
Adapted	The Bernardino Rivadavia Argentine Museum of Natural Sciences has an exceptionally rich fossil collection and runs a scientific institute.
Original	Nearly 50 years later Juan de Garay led a more substantial expedition back to the site, and there, at the mouth of the Rio Riachuelo, he refounded Nuestra Señora Santa Maria del Buen Aire in 1580.
Adapted	Juan de Garay, a Spaniard, led an expedition to the Rio de la Plata region. There, at the mouth of the Rio Riachuelo, he founded the city in 1580.

gorithm. The author compared word use in Newsela and PWKP, showing that the vocabulary is dramatically reduced[5] (50%) in Newsela when comparing the original documents to the more simpler versions, while when comparing vocabulary in the original and simplified version of PWKP the reduction is of only 18%. They also observed that complex syntactic patterns are more often preserved in Simple Wikipedia than in the simplifications of Newsela. An analysis of discourse connectives also revealed than simpler connectives, as suggested by Siddharthan [2003], are more abundant in Newsela than in PWKP.

Moreover, given that Newsela, like Simplext or PortSimples, contains document-level simplification, it allows study of document-level simplification, not just sentence-level simplification.

8.4   NON-ENGLISH TEXT SIMPLIFICATION DATASETS

The Simplext Project developed a parallel corpus of 200 pairs of original and simplified documents. The original documents were provided by the Spanish news agency Servimedia while the manual simplifications were produced by the DILES research group. Simplifications were produced for people with Down Syndrome following a set of recommendations. There was no special tool to support the creation of the simplifications and no links between the original sentences and the simplifications were kept during the text adaptation process. For this reason, an automatic sentence alignment algorithm was developed by Bott and Saggion [2011a], the output of which was corrected by a human editor. In order to facilitate the work of the human corrector, the bi-text GATE editor, a tool which facilitates the task of sentence and word alignment, was used. Each pair of documents was transformed into a GATE XML compound document which contained the original and simplified version together with the automatic alignments. The human editor using the GATE GUI interface corrected the alignments and saved the correct version (see Figure 8.4). Afterward, an XML compliant corpus was produced.

---

[5]Words in the original version which will not show up in the simplified version.

Table 8.4: Examples from the Newsela Corpus. Original is the original text, simp. 1 is the least simplified version and simp. 4 is the strongest simplification

Example	Text Fragments of Four Simplified Versions of the Same Original Text
Original	CHICAGO - On a recent afternoon at Chicago's Dewey Elementary Academy of Fine Arts, Ladon Brumeld asked a group of 9- and 10-year-old African-American girls to define beauty. The nearly 20 girls unanimously agreed that if a woman had short, kinky hair, she was not beautiful. But when Brumeld, the director of a project empowering young girls, passed around a photograph of Lupita Nyong'o, the darkbrown-skinned actress who sports an extra-short natural, the girls were silent for a moment. Then, once again, their answer was unanimous: They agreed Nyong'o was beautiful.
Simp. 1	CHICAGO - On a recent afternoon at a Chicago elementary school, Ladon Brumeld asked a group of 9- and 10-year-old African-American girls to define beauty. The nearly 20 girls unanimously agreed that if a woman had short, kinky hair, she was not beautiful. But then Brumeld, the director of a project empowering young girls, passed around a photograph of Lupita Nyong'o, the dark-brown-skinned actress who wears an extra-short Afro. The girls, who attend Dewey Elementary Academy of Fine Arts, were silent for a moment. Then, once again, their answer was unanimous: They agreed Nyong'o was beautiful.
Simp. 2	CHICAGO - On a recent afternoon, Ladon Brumeld asked a group of 9- and 10-year-old African-American girls to define beauty. The nearly 20 girls unanimously agreed that if a woman had short, kinky hair, she was not beautiful. They thought women with smooth, straight hair were more beautiful. But then Brumeld passed around a picture of Lupita Nyong'o, the dark-skinned actress who wears her hair extrashort. The girls, who attend Dewey Elementary Academy of Fine Arts, were silent for a moment. Then, once again, their answer was unanimous: They agreed Nyong'o was beautiful.
Simp. 3	CHICAGO - On a recent afternoon, a group of 9- and 10-year-old African-American girls talked about beauty. They all agreed that women with short, kinky hair were not beautiful. But then Ladon Brumeld, founder of the group Girls Rule!, passed around a photograph of Lupita Nyong'o. The dark-skinned actress wears her hair extra-short. The girls were silent for a moment. Then, once again, they all agreed: Nyong'o was beautiful.
Simp. 4	CHICAGO - Ladon Brumeld asked a group of African-American girls to think about beauty. Brumeld began Girls Rule!, a girl empowerment project. The girls agreed that women with short, kinky hair were not beautiful. But then Brumeld passed around a picture of Lupita Nyong'o. She is a famous actress. She has dark skin. And Nyong'o wears her hair extra-short. The girls, who are 9 and 10 years old, were silent. Once again, they all agreed. Nyong'o was beautiful.

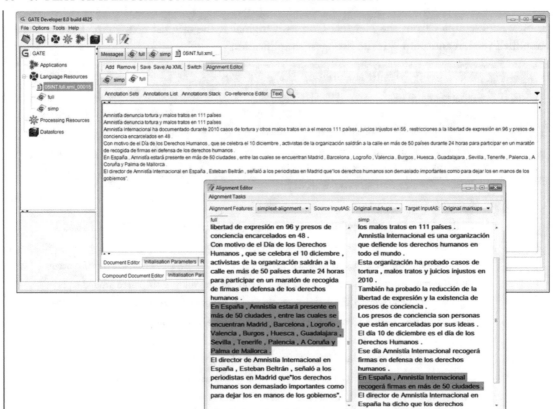

Figure 8.4: Pair of documents (original, simplified) aligned (GATE bi-text alignment editor).

The original documents after being automatically analysed contain: 1,149 sentences (5.7 sentences on average per document) and 40,120 tokens (around 200 tokens per document and 36 tokens per sentence). After automatic processing, the simplified documents contain 1,808 sentences (or an average of 9 sentences per document), 26,546 tokens (or an average of 133 per document with around 15 tokens per sentence).

With respect to the alignments present in the corpus, most of them are one-to-one alignments representing cases where a sentence in the original document is "copied" as is to the simplification or where the simplified sentence is different from the original in some respect. Examples (2) and (3) in Table 8.5 illustrate these cases. Example (1) shows a 1-to-2 alignment; the transformation is not straightforward since it has a certain degree of interpretation in that the qualifier "Bachelor of Fine Arts by University of Valencia" of "Ana Juan" presupposes that "Ana Juan" studied at University of Valencia, therefore making possible to simplify the sentence as it is presented.

Table 8.5: Simplext corpus alignment examples (with free translations in English)

Example	Original	Simplified
1	*Licenciada en Bellas Artes por la Universidad Politécnica de Valencia, Ana Juan es ilustradora, escritora y pintora.* (Bachelor of Fine Arts from the Polytechnic University of Valencia, Ana Juan is an illustrator, writer and painter.)	*Ana Juan es ilustradora, escritora y pintora. Estudió Bellas Artes en la universidad de Valencia.* (Ana Juan is an illustrator, writer and painter. She studied Fine Arts at the University of Valencia.)
2	*La ONU celebra en 2011 el Año Internacional de la Química para fomentar el interés de los jóvenes por esta ciencia y mostrar cómo, gracias a ella, se puede "responder a las necesidades del mundo."* (The UN celebrates in 2011 the International Year of Chemistry to promote the interest of young people in this science and show how, thanks to it, we can meet the needs of the world.)	*En 2011 se celebra el Año Internacional de la Química.* (2011 marks the International Year of Chemistry.)
3	*2011, AÑO INTERNACIONAL DE LA QUÍMICA.* (2011, International Year of Chemistry.)	*El 2011 es el Año Internacional de la Química.* (2011 is the International Year of Chemistry.)
4	*El jugador del Fútbol Club Barcelona Andrés Iniesta colaborará de nuevo con la Federación Española de Enfermedades Raras y pondrá cara a su campaña de sensibilización de 2011.* (A Barcelona Football Club player Andres Iniesta will collaborate again with the Spanish Federation for Rare Diseases and will give his image in the 2011 awareness campain.)	*Andrés Iniesta ayudará este año a la Federacion Española de Enfermedades Raras. Andrés Iniesta es jugador de fútbol en el Futbol Club Barcelona. También prestará su imagen a la campaña de esta Federación.* (Andres Iniesta will help this year the Spanish Federation for Rare Diseases. Andres Iniesta is football player in the Football Club Barcelona. He will also lend his image to the campaign of the Federation.)

Example (4) shows a 1-to-3 alignment where both syntactic and lexical simplifications occur. The complex noun phrase "Barcelona Football Club player Andres Iniesta" is expressed in a single sentence. The coordinated structure in the original sentence ("... will collaborate... and will give his image...") is split into two independent sentences.

The following alignment statistics hold in the Simplext corpus: 552 (38%) 1-to-1 alignments, 258 (18%) 1-to-2 alignments, 99 (7%) 1-to-n alignments (with $n > 2$), 179 (12%) 1-to-0 alignents, 336 (23%) 0-to-1 alignments and finally, only 10 (1%) 2-to-1 alignments. As these statistics show, 1-to-1 transformations with possible content reduction are particularly important, followed by elimination of information (1-to-0 alignments), introduction of definitions (0-to-1 alignmments), and splitting (1-to-2 alignments).

The types of modification range from moderate edits to very complex paraphrasing and although a typology of transformations was attempted by Bott and Saggion [2011b], many cases are extremely complex to fit in any editing pattern; moreover, most edits are the result of jointly applying a number of transformations, complicating the process of describing the exact nature of the transformation.

8.5   EVALUATION

The output of text simplification systems is commonly evaluated by human judgments of its grammaticality (fluency), meaning preservation (adequacy), and simplicity, e.g., [Coster and Kauchak, 2011, Feblowitz and Kauchak, 2013, Siddharthan and Mandya, 2014, Wubben et al., 2012]. Fluency measures grammatical correctness of the output, simplicity measures how simple the output is, and the meaning preservation measures how well the meaning of the simplified sentence corresponds to the meaning of the original sentence. All three scores are usually given on a five-point Likert scale, the exceptions being [Narayan and Gardent, 2014] with a 0–5 scale, and [Glavaš and Štajner, 2013] with a 1–3 scale. In all cases, the higher score indicates the better output.

A second line of evaluation research concentrates on the use of readability indices (see Chapter 2 for past and current research on this issue). A proper methodology of simplification using these metrics was put forward in Drndarević et al. [2013] and further assessed in Štajner and Saggion [2013a]. Works which attempt to evaluate isolated sentences using readability metrics have no sound basis for doing so [Coster and Kauchak, 2011, Woodsend and Lapata, 2011, Zhu et al., 2010], since readability indices are designed for long units such as full texts.

Recently, many studies which propose simplification as machine translation naturally include an additional assessment of the systems' output by comparing it with the gold standard manual simplifications, borrowing the MT evaluation metrics such as BLEU (as, for example, in Coster and Kauchak [2011], Feblowitz and Kauchak [2013], Narayan and Gardent [2014], Specia [2010], Vu et al. [2014], Woodsend and Lapata [2011], Wubben et al. [2012], Zhu et al. [2010]), TERp (as in Vu et al. [2014], Woodsend and Lapata [2011]), and NIST (as in Specia [2010], and Vu et al. [2014]).

BLEU [Papineni et al., 2002] is the most widely used MT evaluation metric which measures similarity between the system's output and a human reference. It is based on exact n-gram matching and heavily penalizes word reordering and sentence shortening. The metric has been found to highly correlate with human judgement in machine translation, being at the same time reliable even when run on different documents and against different numbers of model references. It is based on a "weighted average of similar length phrase matches" (n-grams), it is sensitive to longer n-grams (the baseline being the use of up to 4-grams) and it also includes a brevity penalty factor for penalizing translations shorter than the "gold standard" [Papineni et al., 2002]. Although specifically designed for machine translation, the metric has been applied to evaluate summarization systems [Pastra and Saggion, 2003] and has heavily applied in text simplification evaluation.

The formula for computing the BLEU score is as follows:

$$Bleu(S, R) = K(S, R) * e^{Bleu_1(S,R)} \tag{8.1}$$

$$Bleu_1(S, R) = \sum_{i=1,2,\dots n} w_i * \lg\left(\frac{|(S_i \cap R_i)|}{|S_i|}\right) \tag{8.2}$$

$$K(S, R) = \begin{cases} 1 & \text{if } |S| > |R| \\ e^{(1-\frac{|R|}{|S|})} & \text{otherwise} \end{cases} \tag{8.3}$$

$$w_i = \frac{i}{\sum_{j=1,2,\dots n} j} \qquad \text{for } i = 1, 2, \dots, n, \tag{8.4}$$

where S and R are the system and reference sets. S_i and R_i are the "bags" of i-grams for system and reference. n is the size of the n-gram used.

NIST [Doddington, 2002] is, like BLEU, based on exact n-gram matching, with the difference that it gives different weights to different n-grams (depending on how likely they are to occur) and that its brevity penalty is less severe (small differences in the length of the system's output and the human reference do not impact the overall score as much as in BLEU). TERp [Snover et al., 2009] measures the number of "edits" needed to transform the MT output (simplified version of the original sentence in our case) into the reference translation (original sentence in our case). TERp is an extension of TER—Translation Edit Rate [Snover et al., 2006] that uses phrasal substitutions (using automatically generated paraphrases), stemming, synonyms, relaxed shifting constraints, and other improvements [Snover et al., 2009]. The higher the value of TERp (and each of its components), the less similar the original and its corresponding simplified sentence are.

An additional metric which could be applied in simplification is ROUGE [Lin and Hovy, 2003], a recall metric which also considers n-grams as units for comparing system generated texts to human-generated texts. This could be reasonable in a context where the original text is considerably reduced by recurring text condensation techiques. The ROUGE formula as specified by Lin [2004] is as follows:

$$\text{ROUGE-n(Automatic,Humans)} = \frac{\sum_{I \in \text{Humans}} \sum_{\text{n-gram} \in \text{Automatic}} \text{count}_{\text{match}}(\text{n-gram}))}{\sum_{I \in \text{Humans}} \sum \text{count(n-gram)}},$$

where Automatic is the machine generated text to be evaluated, Humans is the set of ideal human generated texts, $\text{count}_{\text{match}}$ is the number of common n-grams in I (an ideal human summary) and Automatic, and count is the number of n-grams in the human texts. ROUGE has not been tested yet in text simplification evaluation.

8.6   TOWARD AUTOMATICALLY MEASURING THE QUALITY OF SIMPLIFIED OUTPUT

The shared task on quality assessment for text simplification [Štajner et al., 2016] focused on systems able to predict the quality of a simplified text so that such systems could eventually be used in place of human evaluation based on meaning preservation, grammaticality, and simplicity of the generated output. The organizers prepared three datasets of original and simplified sentences from different sources: (i) 272 pairs of sentences from the corpus and system described by Glavaš and Štajner [2013] (see Chapter 3); (ii) 119 pairs of sentences from *Encyclopedia Britannica* and their simplification obtained by Machine Translation–based simplifiers (see Chapter 5); and (iii) 240 pairs of sentence from English Wikipedia lexically simplified by several systems. All the sentence pairs were evaluated by assessing their grammaticality (G), meaning preservation (M), and simplicity (S) using three labels: bad, ok, and good. An overall evaluation (O) was also produced which combines the three different aspects so that the O value will be good when G, M, and S are all good. Two different types of output were proposed by the organizers: in the raw scores task, the systems had to produce a score for each sentence pair; in the classification task, the systems had to produce one class (good, ok, bad) for each sentence pair. The performance of the quality assessment systems was measured using Pearson's correlation coefficient (for the raw scores task) and (i) accuracy, (ii) mean absolute error, (iii) root mean squared error, and (iv) weighted F-score for the classification task. Eight research teams participated in the evaluation. Concerning the raw scores task, the best system [Nisioi and Nauze, 2016] combines an ensemble method (see Dietterich [2000] for an overview) with a recurrent neural network (see Bengio et al. [2003] for example). The ensemble is made of a number of classifiers (SVMs, Logistic Regression, Gradient Boosting Tree, etc.) trained on features which include character n-grams, sentiment information, POS tags, NP chunks, readability indices, negation, etc. The final system is optimized based on particle swarm optimization [Kennedy and Eberhart, 1995]. The recurrent neural network is trained to model relatedness between original and simplified sentences using GloVe vectors [Pennington et al., 2014] trained on dependency parse trees following [Tai et al., 2015]. For the classification task, the best system [Štajner et al., 2016] used a set of 22 machine translation evaluation metrics and 17 quality estimation baseline features, which were used to compare the original sentence with its simplification. The machine learning algorithm used was Random Forest.

8.7   CONCLUSION

As in any other research area of natural language processing, evaluation is a complicated issue. There is currently no agreed approach on how simplification systems should be evaluated and, naturally, many works follow the methodologies which have been applied in previous works, which might not be sound. One issue that complicates evaluation in text simplification research is the fact that data (particularly aligned data) is generally not manually annotated with linguistic information so as to allow tools to be tested in perfect input conditions so as to provide upper bounds for learning simplification transformations. Both lexical and syntactic simplification evaluation data is still scarce and not diverse enough to account for simplification phenomena in different domains or for different target populations. There is certainly lot of work to be done in this specific area; techniques which take advantage of available simplification data and large volumes of non-simplified text have an important role to play. As we have seen in Chapter 2, a considerable number of datasets exist for the study of readability assessment. These datasets could be also considered valuable resources for text simplification evaluation or for the semi-automatic acquisition of further data.

8.8   FURTHER READING

The reader may find it interesting to examine current work on the creation of aligned comparable simplification corpora using current word-embedding models [Kajiwara and Komachi, 2016] as well as work on non-English datasets such as the Italian parallel corpus PaCCSS-IT [Brunato et al., 2016] which contains over 63,000 pairs of sentences (automatically classified into readability levels) harvested from an available corpus. Where available graded resources are of concern, the Age-of-Acquisition norms [Kuperman et al., 2012] is also a useful resource containing, for a set of 51,715 English words, the ratings of the age at which those words were learned.

CHAPTER 9

Conclusion

In recent years, automatic text simplification has attracted the attention of researchers in natural language processing. Research is improving steadily. It is a difficult task for human editors to produce a text that will match the reading abilities of a target population. Therefore, it is an even more difficult task for machines, which are, for the time being, deprived of the necessary linguistic and world knowledge. However, by addressing such an important societal challenge, researchers have created new methods and repurposed old ones. In this book, we have partially covered three relevant simplification topics: text readability, lexical simplification, and syntactic simplification.

Traditional text readability studies have proposed a number of formulas to compute the complexity or grade level of a given text by using a number of easy-to-compute features such as sentence length and word "complexity" (e.g., syllable count). In recent years, however, natural language processing has delved into the problem proposing new ways to better assess the difficulty of text corpora. This was possible thanks to the maturity of tools such as part-of-speech taggers and syntactic parsers which allow us to automatically extract rich features from corpora. Readability formulas have been used in text simplification as either an evaluation measure which informs about the simplicity of the generated output, or as a target function to inform an optimization problem. However, not all studies meet the formulas' requirements; indeed, readability formulas are designed to assess text difficulty, not individual sentence readability or readability of a set of unrelated sentences; therefore, additional research is needed to adapt readability formulas for their use in text simplification evaluation.

Lexical simplification, the task of replacing complex words by easier synonyms, has traditionally relied on the availability of a lexical resource such as a dictionary of synonyms or a thesaurus in order to find suitable substitutes for a given word, a word complexity assessment procedure to identify complex words, and a mechanism to select the most appropriate and simpler synonym in context. Needless to say, an appropriate component for generating correct words is needed to deal with aspects such as agreement. Recent work has taken advantage of the availability of comparable articles to learn lexical simplification rules, but their coverage is limited as complicated words never seen in corpora would never be simplified and valid substitutions will never occur.

Where syntactic simplification is concerned, there are currently three different approaches being adopted in order to address the problem: rule-based systems, trainable systems, and hybrid systems. Rule-based approaches are either based on a corpus study aiming at isolating a possible set of transformations occurring during text simplification, which are then implemented in a computational procedure, or a study of sources of text difficulty is undertaken in order to identify linguistic phenomena affecting readability or comprehensibility and how they can be paraphrased. The advantage of this approach is that the developer can easily generalize observed phenomena or implement phenomena not seen in a corpus yet likely to occur. Trainable systems in text simplification ideally require a parallel corpus of original and simplified sentences. This is not always possible to find; in fact, true parallel simplification corpora are very scarce. Although attempts to learn simplification rules have been known for a long time, it was not until recently that, with the availability of Simple English Wikipedia, simplification as statistical machine translation has taken a center stage in the field. However, the approach is far from delivering good quality simplification as rule-based systems do, since complicated syntactic transformations cannot be captured by approaches which lack syntactic and semantic information known to be necessary for appropriate sentence generation for example. Most current machine translation-based simplification systems can only cover local lexical transformations and some phrase reordering phenomena, in many cases leaving most of the original complex sentence untouched. Hybrid approaches take advantage of both methods; on the one hand they use hand-crafted rules to cover sentence level, complex syntactic phenomena, while on the other hand taking advantage of parallel or comparable corpora to learn more local transformations.

Both lexical simplification and syntactic simplification approaches still lack appropriate models for the intended reader: what is easy for a given individual might be complicated for someone else. Therefore, more research is required on the users' side to understand what their true needs are.

Text simplification can learn from several natural language processing problems such as summarization, text generation, and in particular paraphrase generation, sentence compression, and machine translation. The study of content selection from summarization can help simplification in selecting key propositional content discarding unnecessary elements which could be safely omitted without altering too much the message of the original text.

Appropriate text-to-text generation is needed in simplification in order to produce complete grammatical sentences out of text fragments; moreover, in order to produce a coherent and cohesive text, text planning techniques which have been many times ignored in text simplification are also required.

Text simplification still needs an appropriate evaluation framework with metrics carefully designed for the task.

Although our techniques are still imperfect, text simplification has the potential for taking natural language processing out of the laboratory with real applications that could make a difference for many people in need.

Bibliography

Eneko Agirre and Aitor Soroa. Personalizing PageRank for word sense disambiguation. In *Proc. of the 12th Conference of the European Chapter of the Association for Computational Linguistics*, pages 33–41. Association for Computational Linguistics, 2009. DOI: 10.3115/1609067.1609070. 25

Sandra Aluísio, Lucia Specia, Caroline Gasperin, and Carolina Scarton. Readability assessment for text simplification. In *Proc. of the NAACL HLT 5th Workshop on Innovative use of NLP for Building Educational Applications*, pages 1–9, Stroudsburg, PA, 2010. Association for Computational Linguistics. 69

Sandra Maria Aluísio and Caroline Gasperin. Fostering digital inclusion and accessibility: The PorSimples project for simplification of Portuguese texts. In *Proc. of the NAACL HLT Young Investigators Workshop on Computational Approaches to Languages of the Americas*, pages 46–53, Stroudsburg, PA, 2010. Association for Computational Linguistics. 1, 47, 67

Marcelo Adriano Amancio and Lucia Specia. An analysis of crowd sourced text simplifications. In *Proc. of the 3rd Workshop on Predicting and Improving Text Readability for Target Reader Populations*, PITR, pages 123–130, Gothenburg, Sweden, 2014. DOI: 10.3115/v1/w14-1214. 58

Jonathan Anderson. Analysing the readability of English and non-English texts in the classroom with Lix. In *Proc. of the Annual Meeting of the Australian Reading Association*, 1981. 19, 56

Ángel Alberto Anula Rebollo. Lecturas adaptadas a la enseñanza del español como L2: variables lingüísticas para la determinación del nivel de legibilidad. In *La Evaluación en el Aprendizaje y la Enseñanza del Español como LE/L2*, Pastor y Roca (Eds.), pages 162–170, 2008. 19

Ángel Alberto Anula Rebollo. Tipos de textos, complejidad lingüística y facilitación lectora. In *Actas del Sexto Congreso de Hispanistas de Asia*, pages 45–61, 2009. 67

María Jesús Aranzabe, Arantza Díaz de Ilarraza, and Itziar Gonzalez-Dios. First approach to automatic text simplification in Basque. In *Proc. of the 1st Workshop on Natural Language Processing for Improving Textual Accessibility*, NLP4ITA, pages 1–8, 2012. 1

Niraj Aswani, Valentin Tablan, Kalina Bontcheva, and Hamish Cunningham. Indexing and querying linguistic metadata and document content. In Nicolas Nicolov, Kalina Bontcheva, Galia Angelova, and Ruslan Mitkov, Eds., *Recent Advances in Natural Language Processing IV:*

Selected Papers from RANLP 2005, volume 292 of *Current Issues in Linguistic Theory*, pages 35–44. John Benjamins, Amsterdam & Philadelphia, 2007. DOI: 10.1075/cilt.292. 39

Ricardo A. Baeza-Yates, Luz Rello, and Julia Dembowski. CASSA: A context-aware synonym simplification algorithm. In *Proc. of the Conference of the North American Chapter of the Association for Computational Linguistics (NAACL)*, pages 1380–1385, Denver, Colorado, May 31–June 5, 2015. DOI: 10.3115/v1/n15-1156. 83

Eduard Barbu, Maria Teresa Martín-Valdivia, and Luis Alfonso Ureña López. Open book: A tool for helping ASD users' semantic comprehension. In *Proc. of the Workshop on Natural Language Processing for Improving Textual Accessibility*, NLP4ITA, pages 11–19, Atlanta, Georgia, June 2013. Association for Computational Linguistics. 72

Gianni Barlacchi and Sara Tonelli. ERNESTA: A sentence simplification tool for children's stories in Italian. In *Proc. of the 14th International Conference on Intelligent Text Processing and Computational Linguistics*, volume 2 of *CICLING*, pages 476–487, 2013. DOI: 10.1007/978-3-642-37256-8_39. 1, 40, 43

Kathy Barthe, Claire Juaneda, Dominique Leseigneur, Jean-Claude Loquet, Claude Morin, Jean Escande, and Annick Vayrette. GIFAS rationalized French: A controlled language for aerospace documentation in French. *Technical Communication*, 46 (2): 220–229, 1999. 4

Regina Barzilay and Noemie Elhadad. Sentence alignment for monolingual comparable corpora. In *Proc. of the Conference on Empirical Methods in Natural Language Processing*, EMNLP, pages 25–32, Stroudsburg, PA, 2003. Association for Computational Linguistics. DOI: 10.3115/1119355.1119359. 10, 84

Regina Barzilay and Mirella Lapata. Modeling local coherence: An entity-based approach. *Compututational Linguistics*, 34 (1): 1–34, March 2008. ISSN 0891-2017. DOI: 10.1162/coli.2008.34.1.1. 12

Susana Bautista and Horacio Saggion. Making numerical information more accessible: The implementation of a numerical expression simplification system for Spanish. *ITL International Journal of Applied Linguistics*, 165 (2): 299–323, 2014. 29, 67

Susana Bautista, Carlos León, Raquel Hervás, and Pablo Gervás. Empirical identification of text simplification strategies for reading-impaired people. In *European Conference for the Advancement of Assistive Technology*, Maastricht, the Netherlands, September 2011. DOI: 10.3233/978-1-60750-814-4-567. 21

Yoshua Bengio, Réjean Ducharme, Pascal Vincent, and Christian Janvin. A neural probabilistic language model. *Journal of Machine Learning Research*, 3: 1137–1155, March 2003. ISSN 1532-4435. DOI: 10.1007/10985687_6. 92

Rebekah George Benjamin. Reconstructing readability: Recent developments and recommendations in the analysis of text difficulty. *Educational Psychology Review*, 24 (1): 63–88, March 2012. ISSN 1040-726X. DOI: 10.1007/s10648-011-9181-8. 7

Delphine Bernhard, Louis De Viron, Véronique Moriceau, and Xavier Tannier. Question generation for French: Collating parsers and paraphrasing questions. *Dialogue and Discourse*, 3: 43–74, 2012. DOI: 10.5087/dad.2012.203. 77

Or Biran, Samuel Brody, and Noémie Elhadad. Putting it simply: A context-aware approach to lexical simplification. In *Proc. of the 49th Annual Meeting of the Association for Computational Linguistics*, ACL, pages 496–501, Portland, Oregon, 2011. 25, 28

Bernd Bohnet. Efficient parsing of syntactic and semantic dependency structures. In *Proc. of the 13th Conference on Computational Natural Language Learning: Shared Task*, CoNLL, pages 67–72, Stroudsburg, PA, 2009. Association for Computational Linguistics. DOI: 10.3115/1596409.1596421. 39

Bernd Bohnet, Andreas Langjahr, and Leo Wanner. A development environment for an MTT-based sentence generator. DOI: 10.3115/1118253.1118292. 64

Ignacio Bosque Muñoz and Violeta Demonte Barreto. *Gramática Descriptiva de la Lengua Española*. Real Academia Española, 1999. 63

Stefan Bott and Horacio Saggion. An unsupervised alignment algorithm for text simplification corpus construction. In *Proc. of the Workshop on Monolingual Text-To-Text Generation*, pages 20–26, Stroudsburg, PA, 2011a. Association for Computational Linguistics. 60, 86

Stefan Bott and Horacio Saggion. Spanish text simplification: An exploratory study. *Procesamiento del Lenguaje Natural*, 47: 87–95, 2011b. 3, 62, 90

Stefan Bott, Luz Rello, Biljana Drndarević, and Horacio Saggion. Can Spanish be simpler? LexSiS: Lexical simplification for Spanish. *Proc. of the 24th International Conference on Computational Linguistics*, COLING, Mumbai, pages 357–374, 2012. 21, 22, 23

Stefan Bott, Horacio Saggion, and Simon Mille. Text simplification tools for Spanish. In *Proc. of the 8th International Conference on Language Resources and Evaluation*, LREC, pages 1665–1671, 2012. 65

Nadjet Bouayad-Agha, Gerard Casamayor, Gabriela Ferraro, Simon Mille, Vanesa Vidal, and Leo Wanner. Improving the comprehension of legal documentation: The case of patent claims. In *Proc. of the 12th International Conference on Artificial Intelligence and Law*, pages 78–87. ACM, 2009. DOI: 10.1145/1568234.1568244. 76

Thorsten Brants and Alex Franz. Web 1T 5-gram version 1 LDC2006T13. https://catalog.ldc.upenn.edu/LDC2006T13, 2006. 28, 81

Leo Breiman.   Random forests.   *Machine Learning*, 45 (1): 5–32, 2001. DOI: 10.1023/A:1010933404324. 18

Ted Briscoe and John A. Carroll. Developing and evaluating a probabilistic LR parser of part-of-speech and punctuation labels. In *Proc. of the 4th International Workshop on Parsing Technologies*, pages 48–58, Prague, Czech Republic, 1995. 60

Julian Brooke, Vivian Tsang, David Jacob, Fraser Shein, and Graeme Hirst. Building readability lexicons with unannotated corpora. In *Proc. of the 1st Workshop on Predicting and Improving Text Readability for Target Reader Populations*, PITR, pages 33–39, Stroudsburg, PA, 2012. Association for Computational Linguistics. 80

Laetitia Brouwers, Delphine Bernhard, Anne-Laure Ligozat, and Thomas François. Syntactic sentence simplification for French. In *Proc. of the 3rd Workshop on Predicting and Improving Text Readability for Target Reader Populations*, PITR, pages 47–56, Gothenburg, Sweden, April 2014. Association for Computational Linguistics. DOI: 10.3115/v1/w14-1206. 56

Bertram C. Bruce, Ann D. Rubin, and Kathleen S. Starr.   Why readability formulas fail.   *IEEE Transactions on Professional Communication*, PC-42: 50–52, 1981. DOI: 10.1109/tpc.1981.6447826. 9

Dominique Brunato, Andrea Cimino, Felice Dell'Orletta, and Giulia Venturi. PaCCSS-IT: A parallel corpus of complex-simple sentences for automatic text simplification. In *Proc. of the Conference on Empirical Methods in Natural Language Processing*, pages 351–361, Austin, Texas, November 2016. Association for Computational Linguistics. DOI: 10.18653/v1/d16-1034. 93

Alicia Burga, Joan Codina, Gabriela Ferraro, Horacio Saggion, and Leo Wanner. The challenge of syntactic dependency parsing adaptation for the patent domain. In *Proc. of the ESSLI Workshop on Extrinsic Parse Improvement*, 2013. 76

Christopher J. C. Burges.   A tutorial on support vector machines for pattern recognition. *Data Mining Knowledge Discovery*, 2 (2): 121–167, June 1998.   ISSN 1384-5810. DOI: 10.1023/A:1009715923555. 79

Jill Burstein, John Sabatini, Jane Shore, Brad Moulder, and Jennifer Lentini. A user study: Technology to increase teachers' linguistic awareness to improve instructional language support for English language learners. In *Proc. of the Workshop on Natural Language Processing for Improving Textual Accessibility*, NLP4ITA, pages 1–10, Atlanta, Georgia, June 2013. Association for Computational Linguistics. 77

Chris Callison-Burch, Philipp Koehn, Christof Monz, and Omar Zaidan. Findings of the 2011 Workshop on Statistical Machine Translation. In *Proc. of the 6th Workshop on Statistical Machine Translation*, pages 22–64, 2011. DOI: 10.3115/1626431.1626433. 28

Yvonne Canning, John Tait, Jackie Archibald, and Ros Crawley. Cohesive generation of syntactically simplified newspaper text. In Petr Sojka, Ivan Kopecek, and Karel Pala, Eds., *Text, Speech and Dialogue*, volume 1902 of *Lecture Notes in Computer Science*, pages 145–150. Springer Berlin Heidelberg, 2000. DOI: 10.1007/978-3-642-15760-8. 59

John Carroll, Guido Minnen, Yvonne Canning, Siobhan Devlin, and John Tait. Practical simplification of English newspaper text to assist aphasic readers. In *Proc. of the AAAI'98 Workshop on Integrating AI and Assistive Technology*, pages 7–10, 1998. 1, 4, 21, 23, 24, 28, 59, 75

Celex. The CELEX lexical database. Centre for Lexical Information, Max Planck Institute for Psycholinguistics, 1993. 14

R. Chandrasekar and B. Srinivas. Automatic induction of rules for text simplification. *Knowledge-based Systems*, 10: 183–190, 1997. DOI: 10.1016/s0950-7051(97)00029-4. 34

R. Chandrasekar, Christine Doran, and B. Srinivas. Motivations and methods for text simplification. In *16th International Conference on Computational Linguistics*, pages 1041–1044, 1996. DOI: 10.3115/993268.993361. 1, 33, 40, 73

Eugene Charniak. A maximum-entropy-inspired parser. In *Proc. of the 1st North American Chapter of the Association for Computational Linguistics Conference*, NAACL, pages 132–139, Stroudsburg, PA, 2000. Association for Computational Linguistics. 11

Kenneth Ward Church and Patrick Hanks. Word association norms, mutual information, and lexicography. *Computational Linguistics*, 16 (1): 22–29, March 1990. ISSN 0891-2017. DOI: 10.3115/981623.981633. 14

James Clarke and Mirella Lapata. Models for sentence compression: A comparison across domains, training requirements and evaluation measures. In *Proc. of the 21st International Conference on Computational Linguistics and the 44th Annual Meeting of the Association for Computational Linguistics*, ACL, pages 377–384, Stroudsburg, PA, 2006. Association for Computational Linguistics. DOI: 10.3115/1220175.1220223. 45

Kevyn Collins-Thompson. Computational assessment of text readability. A survey of current and future research. *ITL International Journal of Applied Linguistics*, 165 (2): 97–135, 2014. DOI: 10.1075/itl.165.2.01col. 7, 8

Kevyn Collins-Thompson and James P. Callan. A language modeling approach to predicting reading difficulty. In *Proc. of the Human Language Technology Conference of the North American Chapter of the Association for Computational Linguistics*, NAACL, pages 193–200, 2004. 13, 14

Kevyn Collins-Thompson, Paul N. Bennett, Ryen W. White, Sebastian de la Chica, and David Sontag. Personalizing Web search results by reading level. In *Proc. of the 20th ACM Conference on Information and Knowledge Management, CIKM 2011, Glasgow, October 24–28, 2011*, pages 403–412, 2011. DOI: 10.1145/2063576.2063639. 14, 16

Andrew M. Colman. *Oxford Dictionary of Psychology (On-line Version)*, 4th ed., Oxford University Press, New York, 2016. 72

William Coster and David Kauchak. Learning to simplify sentences using Wikipedia. In *Proc. of the Workshop on Monolingual Text-To-Text Generation*, pages 1–9, Stroudsburg, PA, 2011. Association for Computational Linguistics. 25, 48, 49, 81, 90

Scott A. Crossley, David F. Dufty, Philip M. McCarthy, and Danielle S. McNamara. Toward a new readability: A mixed model approach. *Proc. of the 29th Annual Conference of the Cognitive Science Society*, pages 197–202, 2007. 13

David Crystal. *The Cambridge Encyclopedia of Language*, 1st ed., Cambridge University Press, Cambridge, UK, 1987. 4

Hamish Cunningham, Diana Maynard, and Valentin Tablan. JAPE: A Java annotation patterns engine (2nd ed.). Research Memorandum CS-00-10, Department of Computer Science, University of Sheffield, November 2000. 30, 39, 64

James Curran, Stephen Clark, and Johan Bos. Linguistically motivated large-scale NLP with C&C and Boxer. In *Proc. of the 45th Annual Meeting of the Association for Computational Linguistics Companion Volume Proceedings of the Demo and Poster Sessions*, ACL, pages 33–36, Prague, Czech Republic, June 2007. Association for Computational Linguistics. DOI: 10.3115/1557769.1557781. 57

Edgar Dale and Jeanne S. Chall. A formula for predicting readability. *Educational Research Bulletin*, 27 (1): 11–28, 1948a. ISSN 15554023. 9

Edgar Dale and Jeanne S. Chall. The concept of readability. *Elementary English*, 23 (24), 1948b. 7

Alice Davison, Robert N. Kantor, Jean Hannah Kantor, Gabriela Hermon, Richard Lutz, and Robert Salzillo. Limitations of readability formulas in guiding adaptations of texts. Technical Report 162, University of Illinois Center for the Study of Reading, Urbana, 1980. 9

Jan De Belder. *Integer Linear Programming for Natural Language Processing*. Ph.D. thesis, Informatics Section, Department of Computer Science, Faculty of Engineering Science, March 2014. 9, 55

Jan De Belder and Marie-Francine Moens. A dataset for the evaluation of lexical simplification. In Alexander Gelbukh, Ed., *Computational Linguistics and Intelligent Text Processing*, volume 7182 of *Lecture Notes in Computer Science*, pages 426–437. Springer, Berlin Heidelberg, 2012. DOI: 10.1007/978-3-540-70939-8. 81, 82

Jan De Belder, Koen Deschacht, and Marie-Francine Moens. Lexical simplification. In *Proc. of the 1st International Conference on Interdisciplinary Research on Technology, Education and Communication*, Kortrijk, Belgium, May 25–27, 2010. 26

Felice Dell'Orletta, Simonetta Montemagni, and Giulia Venturi. READ-IT: Assessing readability of Italian texts with a view to text simplification. In *Proc. of the 2nd Workshop on Speech and Language Processing for Assistive Technologies*, SLPAT, pages 73–83, Stroudsburg, PA, 2011. Association for Computational Linguistics. 1

Felice Dell'Orletta, Simonetta Montemagni, and Giulia Venturi. Assessing document and sentence readability in less resourced languages and across textual genres. *Special Issue of the International Journal of Applied Linguistics*, 165 (2): 163–193, 2014a. DOI: 10.1075/itl.165.2.03del. 16

Felice Dell'Orletta, Martijn Wieling, Giulia Venturi, Andrea Cimino, and Simonetta Montemagni. Assessing the readability of sentences: Which corpora and features? In *Proc. of the 9th Workshop on Innovative use of NLP for Building Educational Applications*, pages 163–173, Baltimore, Maryland, June 2014b. Association for Computational Linguistics. DOI: 10.3115/v1/w14-1820. 16

A. P. Dempster, M. N. Laird, and D. B. Rubin. Maximum likelihood from incomplete data via the EM algorithm. *Journal of the Royal Statistical Society: Series B (Statistical Methodology)*, 39: 1–22, 1977. 57

Siobhan Devlin and John Tait. The use of a psycholinguistic database in the simplification of text for aphasic readers. *Linguistic Databases*, pages 161–173, 1998. 59

Siobhan Devlin and Gary Unthank. Helping aphasic people process online information. In *Proc. of the 8th International ACM SIGACCESS Conference on Computers and Accessibility*, pages 225–226, New York, 2006. ACM. DOI: 10.1145/1168987.1169027. 3, 4, 60

Thomas G. Dietterich. Ensemble methods in machine learning. In *Proc. of the 1st International Workshop on Multiple Classifier Systems*, pages 1–15, London, UK, 2000. Springer-Verlag. DOI: 10.1007/3-540-45014-9_1. 92

Yuan Ding and Martha Palmer. Machine translation using probabilistic synchronous dependency insertion grammars. In *Proc. of the 43rd Annual Meeting on Association for Computational Linguistics*, ACL, pages 541–548, Stroudsburg, PA, 2005. Association for Computational Linguistics. DOI: 10.3115/1219840.1219907. 37

George Doddington. Automatic evaluation of machine translation quality using n-gram cooccurrence statistics. In *Proc. of the 2nd Conference on Human Language Technology Research*, pages 138–145, San Diego, 2002. DOI: 10.3115/1289189.1289273. 91

Mark Dras. *Tree Adjoining Grammar and the Reluctant Paraphrasing of Text*. Ph.D. thesis, Macquarie University, 1999. 45

Biljana Drndarević and Horacio Saggion. Reducing text complexity through automatic lexical simplification: An empirical study for Spanish. *Procesamiento del Lenguaje Natural*, 49: 13–20, 2012a. 3, 63

Biljana Drndarević and Horacio Saggion. Towards automatic lexical simplification in Spanish: An empirical study. In *Proc. of the 1st Workshop on Predicting and Improving Text Readability for Target Reader Populations*, PITR, pages 8–16, Montréal, Canada, June 2012b. Association for Computational Linguistics. 3, 62

Biljana Drndarević, Sanja Štajner, and Horacio Saggion. Reporting simply: A lexical simplification strategy for enhancing text accessibility. In *Proc. of the Easy-to-read on the Web Symposium*, 2012. 63

Biljana Drndarević, Sanja Štajner, Stefan Bott, Susana Bautista, and Horacio Saggion. Automatic text simplification in Spanish: A comparative evaluation of complementing modules. In *Proc. of the 14th International Conference on Computational Linguistics and Intelligent Text Processing*, pages 488–500, 2013. DOI: 10.1007/978-3-642-37256-8_40. 63, 90

William H. DuBay. The principles of readability. *Impact Information*, pages 1–76, 2004. 7, 8

Jason Eisner. Learning non-isomorphic tree mappings for machine translation. In *Proc. of the 41st Annual Meeting of the Association for Computational Linguistics*, ACL, pages 205–208. The Association for Computational Linguistics, 2003. DOI: 10.3115/1075178.1075217. 55

Noemie Elhadad. Comprehending technical texts: Predicting and defining unfamiliar terms. In *AMIA Annual Symposium Proceedings*, pages 239–243, 2006. 31

Maxine Eskenazi, Yibin Lin, and Oscar Saz. Tools for non-native readers: The case for translation and simplification. In *Proc. of the Workshop on Natural Language Processing for Improving Textual Accessibility*, NLP4ITA, pages 20–28, Atlanta, Georgia, June 2013. Association for Computational Linguistics. 77

Richard Evans, Constantin Orasan, and Iustin Dornescu. An evaluation of syntactic simplification rules for people with autism. In *Proc. of the 3rd Workshop on Predicting and Improving Text Readability for Target Reader Populations*, PITR, pages 131–140, Gothenburg, Sweden, April 2014. Association for Computational Linguistics. DOI: 10.3115/v1/w14-1215. 72

Richard J. Evans. Comparing methods for the syntactic simplification of sentences in information extraction. *Literary and Linguistic Computing*, 26 (4): 371–388, 2011. DOI: 10.1093/llc/fqr034. 74

Inmaculada Fajardo, Vicenta Ávila, Antonio Ferrer, Gema Tavares, Marcos Gómez, and Ana Hernández. Easy-to-read texts for students with intellectual disability: Linguistic factors affecting comprehension. *Journal of Applied Research in Intellectual Disabilities*, 27 (3): 212–225, 2014. ISSN 1468-3148. DOI: 10.1111/jar.12065. 4

Manaal Faruqui, Jesse Dodge, Sujay Kumar Jauhar, Chris Dyer, Eduard Hovy, and Noah A. Smith. Retrofitting word vectors to semantic lexicons. In *Proc. of the Conference of the North American Chapter of the Association for Computational Linguistics: Human Language Technologies*, NAACL, pages 1606–1615, Denver, Colorado, May–June 2015. Association for Computational Linguistics. DOI: 10.3115/v1/n15-1184. 27

Dan Feblowitz and David Kauchak. Sentence simplification as tree transduction. In *Proc. of the 2nd Workshop on Predicting and Improving Text Readability for Targe Reader Populations*, PITR, pages 1–10, Sofia, Bulgaria, 2013. 90

Lijun Feng, Noémie Elhadad, and Matt Huenerfauth. Cognitively motivated features for readability assessment. In *Proc. of the 12th Conference of the European Chapter of the Association for Computational Linguistics*, EACL, pages 229–237, Stroudsburg, PA, 2009. Association for Computational Linguistics. DOI: 10.3115/1609067.1609092. 4, 9, 12, 14

Lijun Feng, Martin Jansche, Matt Huenerfauth, and Noémie Elhadad. A comparison of features for automatic readability assessment. In *Proc. of the 23rd International Conference on Computational Linguistics*, COLING, pages 276–284, Stroudsburg, PA, 2010. Association for Computational Linguistics. 12

Gabriela Ferraro. *Towards deep content extraction from specialized discourse: The case of verbal relations in patent claims*. Ph.D. thesis, Universitat Pompeu Fabra, Barcelona, Spain, 2012. 76

Daniel Ferrés, Monserrat Marimon, and Horacio Saggion. A Web-based text simplification system for English. *Procesamiento del Lenguaje Natural*, 55: 191–194, 2015. 37, 40

Daniel Ferrés, Montserrat Marimon, Horacio Saggion, and Ahmed AbuRa'ed. YATS: Yet another text simplifier. In *Proc. of the 21st International Conference on Applications of Natural Language to Information Systems*, pages 335–342, 2016. DOI: 10.1007/978-3-319-41754-7_32. 37

Katja Filippova and Michael Strube. Sentence fusion via dependency graph compression. In *Proc. of the Conference on Empirical Methods in Natural Language Processing*, EMNLP, pages 177–185, Stroudsburg, PA, 2008. Association for Computational Linguistics. DOI: 10.3115/1613715.1613741. 53

Rudolf Flesch. *The Art of Readable Writing*. Harper, New York, 1949. DOI: 10.2307/1225957. 8

Michael Flor and Beata Beigman Klebanov. Associative lexical cohesion as a factor in text complexity. *ITL—International Journal of Applied Linguistics*, 165 (2): 223–258, 2014. DOI: 10.1075/itl.165.2.05flo. 14

Geert Freyhoff, Gerhard Hess, Linda Kerr, Bror Tronbacke, and Kathy Van Der Veken. *Make it Simple, European Guidelines for the Production of Easy-to-Read Information for People with Learning Disability*. ILSMH European Association, Brussels, 1998. 63

Núria Gala, Thomas François, and Cédrick Fairon. Towards a French lexicon with difficulty measures: NLP helping to bridge the gap between traditional dictionaries and specialized lexicons. In *Proc. of the eLex Conference: Electronic Lexicography in the 21st Century: Thinking Outside the Paper*, Tallinn, Estonia, 2013. DOI: 10.13140/2.1.3913.4089. 79

William A. Gale, Kenneth W. Church, and David Yarowsky. One sense per discourse. In *Proc. of the Workshop on Speech and Natural Language*, pages 233–237, 1992. DOI: 10.3115/1075527.1075579. 23

Caroline Gasperin, Erick Maziero, Lucia Specia, Thiago Pardo, and Sandra M. Aluísio. Natural language processing for social inclusion: A text simplification architecture for different literacy levels. In *Proc. of SEMISH-XXXVI Seminário Integrado de Software e Hardware*, pages 387–401, 2009a. 69, 77

Caroline Gasperin, Lucia Specia, Tiago F. Pereira, and Sandra M. Aluísio. Learning when to simplify sentences for natural text simplification. In *Encontro Nacional de Inteligência Artificial*, pages 809–818, 2009b. 58, 67

Goran Glavaš and Sanja Štajner. Event-centered simplification of news stories. In *Recent Advances in Natural Language Processing, RANLP*, pages 71–78, 2013. 40, 43, 90, 92

Goran Glavaš and Sanja Štajner. Simplifying lexical simplification: Do we need simplified corpora? In *Proc. of the 53rd Annual Meeting of the Association for Computational Linguistics and the 7th International Joint Conference on Natural Language Processing of the Asian Federation of Natural Language Processing*, ACL, pages 63–68, July 26–31, 2015. DOI: /10.3115/v1/p15-2011. 26

Itziar Gonzalez-Dios, Maria Jesús Aranzabe, Arantza Diaz de Ilarraza, and Haritz Salaberri. Simple or complex? Assessing the readability of Basque texts. *Proc. of the 5th International Conference on Computational Linguistics*, pages 334–344, 2014. 19

Arthur C. Graesser, Danielle S. McNamara, Max M. Louwerse, and Zhiqiang Cai. Coh-Metrix: Analysis of text on cohesion and language. *Behavior Research Methods, Instruments, & Computers*, 36 (2): 193–202, May 2004. DOI: 10.3758/bf03195564. 13, 70

Robert Gunning. *The Technique of Clear Writing*. McGraw-Hill, 1952. 9

Mark Hall, Eibe Frank, Geoffrey Holmes, Bernhard Pfahringer, Peter Reutemann, and Ian H. Witten. The WEKA data mining software: An update. *SIGKDD Explorations Newsletter*, 11 (1): 10–18, November 2009. ISSN 1931-0145. DOI: 10.1145/1656274.1656278. 18, 70

Michael A. K. Halliday and Ruqaiya Hasan. *Cohesion in English*. Longman, London, 1976. DOI: 10.4324/9781315836010. 14

Michael Heilman and Noah A. Smith. Good question! Statistical ranking for question generation. In *Proc. of the Annual Conference of the North American Chapter of the Association for Computational Linguistics*, NAACL, pages 609–617, Stroudsburg, PA, 2010. Association for Computational Linguistics. 77

Michael J. Heilman, Kevyn Collins-Thompson, Jamie Callan, and Maxime Eskanazi. Combining lexical and grammatical features to improve readability measures for first and second language texts. In *Proc. of the Human Language Technology Conference of the North American Chapter of the Association for Computational Linguistics*, pages 460–467, 2007. 13

Colby Horn, Cathryn Manduca, and David Kauchak. Learning a lexical simplifier using Wikipedia. In *Proc. of the 52nd Annual Meeting of the Association for Computational Linguistics*, ACL, pages 458–463, 2014. DOI: 10.3115/v1/p14-2075. 24, 26, 27, 81, 83

Kentaro Inui, Atsushi Fujita, Tetsuro Takahashi, Ryu Iida, and Tomoya Iwakura. Text simplification for reading assistance: A project note. In *Proc. of the 2nd International Workshop on Paraphrasing: Paraphrase Acquisition and Applications*, pages 9–16, 2003. DOI: 10.3115/1118984.1118986. 1, 71

Kumar Sujay Jauhar and Lucia Specia. UOW-SHEF: SimpLex—Lexical simplicity ranking based on contextual and psycholinguistic features. In *Proc. of the 6th International Workshop on Semantic Evaluation*, SEMEVAL, pages 477–481. Association for Computational Linguistics, 2012. 27, 28

Thorsten Joachims. Text categorization with support vector machines: Learning with many relevant features. In *Proc. of the 10th European Conference on Machine Learning*, ECML, pages 137–142, London, UK, 1998. Springer-Verlag. DOI: 10.1007/bfb0026683. 3

Thorsten Joachims. Training linear SVMs in linear time. In *Proc. of the 12th ACM SIGKDD International Conference on Knowledge Discovery and Data Mining*, KDD, pages 217–226, New York, 2006. ACM. DOI: 10.1145/1150402.1150429. 81

Siddhartha Jonnalagadda, Luis Tari, Jörg Hakenberg, Chitta Baral, and Graciela Gonzalez. Towards effective sentence simplification for automatic processing of biomedical text. In *Proc. of the 2009 Annual Conference of the North American Chapter of the Association for Computational Linguistics*, NAACL, pages 177–180, Stroudsburg, PA, 2009. Association for Computational Linguistics. DOI: 10.3115/1620853.1620902. 73

Tomoyuki Kajiwara and Mamoru Komachi. Building a monolingual parallel corpus for text simplification using sentence similarity based on alignment between word embeddings. In *Proc. of
the 26th International Conference on Computational Linguistics*, pages 1147–1158, Osaka, Japan,
December 11–16 2016. 93

Hans Kamp. A theory of truth and semantic representation. In J. Groenendijk, T. Janssen, and
M. Stokhof, Eds., *Formal Methods in the Study of Language*. 1981. 57

David Kauchak. Improving text simplification language modeling using unsimplified text data.
In *Proc. of the 51st Annual Meeting of the Association for Computational Linguistics*, ACL,
pages 1537–1546. The Association for Computational Linguistics, 2013. 24, 28

James Kennedy and Russell C. Eberhart.   Particle swarm optimization.   In *Proc. of
the IEEE International Conference on Neural Networks*, pages 1942–1948, 1995. DOI:
10.1109/icnn.1995.488968. 92

A. Keselman, L. Slaughter, C. Arnott-Smith, G. Kim, H. Divita, C. Browne, A. Tsai, and
Q. Zeng-Treitler. Towards consumer-friendly PHRs: Patients experience with reviewing their
health records. In *AMIA Annual Symposium Proceedings*, pages 399–403, 2007. 31

Robin Keskisärkkä. Automatic text simplification via synonym replacement. Master's thesis,
Linköping University, 2012. 21

J. Peter Kincaid, Robert P. Fishburne, Richard L. Rogers, and Brad S. Chissom. Derivation of
new readability formulas (Automated Readability Index, Fog count and Flesch Reading Ease
Formula) for Navy enlisted personnel. Technical report, Naval Technical Training Command,
1975. 8, 12

Beata Beigman Klebanov, Kevin Knight, and Daniel Marcu. Text simplification for information-
seeking applications. In *On the Move to Meaningful Internet Systems 2004: CoopIS, DOA, and
ODBASE, OTM Confederated International Conferences*, pages 735–747, Agia Napa, Cyprus,
October 25–29, 2004. DOI: 10.1007/978-3-540-30468-5_47. 75

Dan Klein and Christopher D. Manning.   Accurate unlexicalized parsing.   In *Proc. of
the 41st Annual Meeting of the Association for Computational Linguistics*, volume 1, ACL,
pages 423–430, Stroudsburg, PA, 2003. Association for Computational Linguistics. DOI:
10.3115/1075096.1075150. 13, 84

Sigrid Klerke and Anders Søgaard. Simple, readable sub-sentences. In *Proc. of the 51st Annual Meeting of the Association for Computational Linguistics—Student Research Workshop*, ACL,
pages 142–149. The Association for Computational Linguistics, 2013. 56

Kevin Knight and Daniel Marcu. Summarization beyond sentence extraction: A probabilistic
approach to sentence compression. *Artificial Intelligence*, 139 (1): 91–107, July 2002. DOI:
10.1016/s0004-3702(02)00222-9. 45

Philipp Koehn, Hieu Hoang, Alexandra Birch, Chris Callison-Burch, Marcello Federico, Nicola Bertoldi, Brooke Cowan, Wade Shen, Christine Moran, Richard Zens, Chris Dyer, Ondřej Bojar, Alexandra Constantin, and Evan Herbst. Moses: Open source toolkit for statistical machine translation. In *Proc. of the 45th Annual Meeting of the Association for Computational Linguistics—Interactive Poster and Demonstration Sessions*, ACL, pages 177–180, Stroudsburg, PA, 2007. Association for Computational Linguistics. DOI: 10.3115/1557769.1557821. 48, 53

Robert Krovetz. More than one sense per discourse. In *NEC Princeton NJ Labs., Research Memorandum*, 1998. 23

Victor Kuperman, Hans Stadthagen-Gonzalez, and Marc Brysbaert. Age-of-acquisition ratings for 30,000 English words. *Behavior Research Methods*, 44 (4): 978–990, 2012. DOI: 10.3758/s13428-012-0210-4. 93

Partha Lal and Stefan Rüger. Extract-based summarization with simplification. In *Proc. of the Document Understanding Conference*, 2002. 21, 75

Thomas K. Landauer and Susan T. Dumais. A solution to Plato's problem: The latent semantic analysis theory of acquisition, induction, and representation of knowledge. *Psychological Review*, 104 (2): 211–240, 1997. DOI: 10.1037//0033-295x.104.2.211. 80

Batia Laufer and Paul Nation. A vocabulary-size test of controlled productive ability. *Language Testing*, 16 (1): 33–51, 1999. DOI: 10.1177/026553229901600103. 18

Alberto Lavelli, Johan Hall, Jens Nilsson, and Joakim Nivre. Maltparser at the EVALITA 2009 dependency parsing task. In *Proc. of EVALITA*, 2009. 43

Benoit Lavoie and Owen Rambow. A fast and portable realizer for text generation systems. In *Proc. of the 5th Conference on Applied Natural Language Processing*, Washington DC, pages 265–268, 1997. DOI: 10.3115/974557.974596. 37

Chin-Yew Lin. ROUGE: A package for automatic evaluation of summaries. In *Proc. of the Workshop on Text Summarization*, Barcelona, 2004. 91

Chin-Yew Lin and Eduard Hovy. Automatic evaluation of summaries using n-gram co-occurrence statistics. In *Proc. of the Human Language Technology Conference of the North American Chapter of the Association for Computational Linguistics*, NAACL, pages 71–78, Edmonton, Canada, 2003. DOI: 10.3115/1073445.1073465. 91

Dekang Lin. Dependency-based evaluation of Minipar. In Anne Abeillé, Ed., *Treebanks: Building and Using Parsed Corpora*, Volume 20, pages 317–329. Springer Netherlands, Dordrecht, 2003. DOI: 10.1007/978-94-010-0201-1. 76

Yuri Lin, Jean-Baptiste Michel, Erez Lieberman Aiden, Jon Orwant, Will Brockman, and Slav Petrov. Syntactic annotations for the Google Books n-gram Corpus. In *Proc. of the ACL System Demonstrations*, pages 169–174, Stroudsburg, PA, 2012. Association for Computational Linguistics. 83

Shervin Malmasi, Mark Dras, and Marcos Zampieri. LTG at SemEval 2016 task 11: Complex word identification with classifier ensembles. In *Proc. of the 10th International Workshop on Semantic Evaluation, (SemEval@NAACL-HLT 2016)*, pages 996–1000, San Diego, CA, June 16–17, 2016. DOI: 10.18653/v1/S16-1154. 25

William C. Mann and Sandra A. Thompson. Rhetorical structure theory: Toward a functional theory of text organization. *Text*, 8 (3): 243–281, 1988. DOI: 10.1515/text.1.1988.8.3.243. 73, 76

Christopher D. Manning, Prabhakar Raghavan, and Hinrich Schütze. *Introduction to Information Retrieval*. Cambridge University Press, 2008. DOI: 10.1017/cbo9780511809071. 10

Montserrat Marimon, Horacio Saggion, and Daniel Ferrés. Porting a methodology for syntactic simplification from English to Spanish. In *Workshop on Replicability and Reproducibility in Natural Language Processing: Adaptive Methods, Resources and Software (IJCAI 2015)*, 2015. 40

Maria Teresa Martín-Valdivia, Eugenio Martínez Cámara, Eduard Barbu, Luis Alfonso Ureña López, Paloma Moreda, and Elena Lloret. Proyecto FIRST (Flexible Interactive Reading Support Tool): Desarrollo de una herramienta para ayudar a personas con autismo mediante la simplificación de textos. *Procesamiento del Lenguaje Natural*, 53: 143–146, 2014. 70, 72

Diana Maynard, Valentin Tablan, Hamish Cunningham, Cristian Ursu, Horacio Saggion, Kalina Bontcheva, and Yorick Wilks. Architectural elements of language engineering robustness. *Natural Language Engineering*, 8 (2/3): 257–274, 2002. DOI: 10.1017/s1351324902002930. 39, 60, 75

Diana McCarthy and Roberto Navigli. The English lexical substitution task. *Language Resources and Evaluation*, 43 (2): 139–159, 2009. DOI: 10.1007/s10579-009-9084-1. 28

Harry G. McLaughlin. SMOG grading—a new readability formula. *Journal of Reading*, pages 639–646, May 1969. 9

Julie Medero and Mari Ostendorf. Identifying targets for syntactic simplification. In *Proc. of the International Workshop on Speech and Language Technology in Education*, pages 69–72, Venice, Italy, August 24–26, 2011. 58

Igor Mel'čuk. *Dependency Syntax: Theory and Practice*. State University of New York Press, 1988. 37

Tomas Mikolov, Wen-tau Yih, and Geoffrey Zweig. Linguistic regularities in continuous space word representations. In *Proc. of the Conference of the North American Chapter of the Association of Computational Linguistics*, NAACL, pages 746–751, Atlanta, Georgia, June 9–14, 2013. 27

George A. Miller, Richard Beckwith, Christiane Fellbaum, Derek Gross, and Katheine J. Miller. Introduction to WordNet: An on-line lexical database. *International Journal of Lexicography*, 3 (4): 235–244, 1990. DOI: 10.1093/ijl/3.4.235. 21, 25

Thomas M. Mitchell. *Machine Learning*, 1st ed., McGraw-Hill, Inc., New York, 1997. 13

Shashi Narayan and Claire Gardent. Hybrid simplification using deep semantics and machine translation. In *Proc. of the 52nd Annual Meeting of the Association for Computational Linguistics*, ACL, pages 435–445, Baltimore, MD, June 22–27, 2014. DOI: 10.3115/v1/p14-1041. 57, 90

Gonzalo Navarro. A guided tour to approximate string matching. *ACM Computer Surveys*, 33 (1): 31–88, March 2001. ISSN 0360-0300. DOI: 10.1145/375360.375365. 49, 57

Sergiu Nisioi and Fabrice Nauze. An ensemble method for quality assessment of text simplification. In *Proc. of the Workshop and Shared Task on Quality Assessment for Text Simplification (QATS)*, Portoroz, Slovenia, 2016. 92

C. F. Norbury. Barking up the wrong tree? Lexical ambiguity resolution in children with language impairments and autistic spectrum disorders. *Journal of Experimental Child Psychology*, 90: 142–171, 2005. DOI: 10.1016/j.jecp.2004.11.003. 4

Franz Josef Och and Hermann Ney. A systematic comparison of various statistical alignment models. *Computational Linguistics*, 29 (1): 19–51, March 2003. ISSN 0891-2017. DOI: 10.1162/089120103321337421. 26

Charles Kay Ogden. *Basic English: A General Introduction with Rules and Grammar*. Paul Treber, London, 1937. 4

Ethel Ong, Jerwin Damay, Gerard Lojico, Kimberly Lu, and Dex Tarantan. Simplifying text in medical literature. *Journal of Research in Science, Computing and Engineering*, 4 (1): 37–47, 2007. DOI: 10.3860/jrsce.v4i1.441. 75

Lluis Padró, Miquel Collado, Samuel Reese, Marina Lloberes, and Irene Castellón. FreeLing 2.1: Five years of open-source language processing tools. In *Proc. of the 7th International Conference on Language Resources and Evaluation*, LREC, Valletta, Malta, May 19–21, 2010. 29

Gustavo Paetzold and Lucia Specia. LEXenstein: A framework for lexical simplification. In *Proc. of the ACL-IJCNLP System Demonstrations*, pages 85–90, Beijing, China, 2015. DOI: 10.3115/v1/p15-4015. 80

Gustavo Paetzold and Lucia Specia. SemEval 2016 Task 11: Complex word identification. In *Proc. of the 10th International Workshop on Semantic Evaluation*, SEMEVAL, pages 560–569, San Diego, California, June 2016a. Association for Computational Linguistics. DOI: 10.18653/v1/S16-1085. 24

Gustavo Paetzold and Lucia Specia. SV000gg at SemEval 2016 task 11: Heavy gauge complex word identification with system voting. In *Proc. of the 10th International Workshop on Semantic Evaluation*, SEMEVAL, pages 969–974, San Diego, CA, June 16–17, 2016b. DOI: 10.18653/v1/S16-1149. 24

Gustavo Henrique Paetzold. *Lexical Simplification for Non-Native English Speakers*. Ph.D. thesis, The University of Sheffield, 2016. 27, 31, 80

João Rafael de Moura Palotti, Guido Zuccon, and Allan Hanbury. The influence of pre-processing on the estimation of readability of Web documents. In *Proc. of the 24th ACM International on Conference on Information and Knowledge Management*, CIKM, pages 1763–1766, New York, 2015. ACM. DOI: 10.1145/2806416.2806613. 15

Kishore Papineni, Salim Roukos, Todd Ward, and Wei-Jing Zhu. BLEU: A method for automatic evaluation of machine translation. In *Proc. of the 40th Annual Meeting of the Association for Computational Linguistics*, ACL, pages 311–318, Stroudsburg, PA, 2002. Association for Computational Linguistics. DOI: 10.3115/1073083.1073135. 48, 91

Katerina Pastra and Horacio Saggion. Colouring summaries BLEU. In *Proc. of the EACL Workshop on Evaluation Initiatives in Natural Language Processing: Are Evaluation Methods, Metrics and Resources Reusable?*, pages 35–42, April 14, 2003. DOI: 10.3115/1641396.1641402. 91

Jeffrey Pennington, Richard Socher, and Christopher D. Manning. GloVe: Global vectors for word representation. In *Proc. of the Conference on Empirical Methods in Natural Language Processing*, EMNLP, pages 1532–1543, Doha, Qatar, October 25–29, 2014. DOI: 10.3115/v1/d14-1162. 26, 27, 92

Sarah E. Petersen and Mari Ostendorf. Text simplification for language learners: A corpus analysis. In *Proc. of the Workshop on Speech and Language Technology in Education*, SLaTE, pages 69–72, Farmington, PA, October 1–3, 2007. 2, 3, 11, 58

Emanuele Pianta, Christian Girardi, and Roberto Zanoli. The TextPro tool suite. In *Proc. of the 6th International Conference on Language Resources and Evaluation*, LREC, Marrakech, Morocco, May 2008. 43

Emily Pitler and Ani Nenkova. Revisiting readability: A unified framework for predicting text quality. In *Proc. of the Conference on Empirical Methods in Natural Language Processing*, EMNLP, pages 186–195, Stroudsburg, PA, 2008. Association for Computational Linguistics. DOI: 10.3115/1613715.1613742. 12

J. Ross Quinlan. *C4.5: Programs for Machine Learning*. Morgan Kaufmann Publishers Inc., San Francisco, CA, 1993. 3

P. Quinlan. *The Oxford Psycholinguistic Database*. Oxford University Press, 1992. DOI: 10.1017/S030500090000941. 21

Randolph Quirk, Sidney Greenbaum, Geoffrey Leech, and Jan Svartvik. *A Comprehensive Grammar of the English Language*. Longman Inc., New York, 1985. 63

Luz Rello. *DysWebxia. A Text Accessibility Model for People with Dyslexia*. Ph.D. thesis, Universitat Pompeu Fabra, Barcelona, Spain, 2014. 72

Luz Rello, Ricardo A. Baeza-Yates, Stefan Bott, and Horacio Saggion. Simplify or help? Text simplification strategies for people with dyslexia. In *Proc. of the International Cross-Disciplinary Conference on Web Accessibility*, W4A, Rio de Janeiro, Brazil, May 13–15, 2013a. DOI: 10.1145/2461121.2461126. 72

Luz Rello, Ricardo A. Baeza-Yates, Laura Dempere-Marco, and Horacio Saggion. Frequent words improve readability and short words improve understandability for people with dyslexia. In *Proc. of the International Conference on Human-Computer Interaction (Part IV)*, INTERACT, pages 203–219, Cape Town, South Africa, September 2–6, 2013b. DOI: 10.1007/978-3-642-40498-6_15. 4, 72

Luz Rello, Susana Bautista, Ricardo A. Baeza-Yates, Pablo Gervás, Raquel Hervás, and Horacio Saggion. One half or 50%? An eye-tracking study of number representation readability. In *Proc. of the International Conference on Human-Computer Interaction (Part IV)*, INTERACT, pages 229–245, Cape Town, South Africa, September 2–6, 2013c. DOI: 10.1007/978-3-642-40498-6_17. 72

José Rodríguez Diéguez, Pilar Moro Berihuete, and Maria Cabero Pérez. Ecuaciones de predicción de lecturabilidad. *Enseñanza: Anuario Interuniversitario de Didáctica*, 10–11: 47–64, 1993. ISSN 2386-3927. 19

Francesco Ronzano, Ahmed AbuRa'ed, Luis Espinosa Anke, and Horacio Saggion. TALN at SemEval 2016 task 11: Modelling complex words by contextual, lexical and semantic features. In *Proc. of the 10th International Workshop on Semantic Evaluation*, SEMEVAL, pages 1011–1016, San Diego, CA, June 16–17, 2016. DOI: 10.18653/v1/S16-1157. 24

Horacio Saggion, Elena Gómez-Martínez, Esteban Etayo, Alberto Anula, and Lorena Bourg. Text simplification in Simplext: Making text more accessible. *Procesamiento del Lenguaje Natural*, 47: 341–342, 2011. 1, 49, 60

Horacio Saggion, Montserrat Marimon, and Daniel Ferrés. Simplificación automática de textos para la accesibilidad de colectivos con discapacidad: Experiencias para el español y el inglés.

In *IX Jornadas Científicas Internacionales de Investigación sobre Personas con Discapacidad*, Salamanca, Spain, 2015a. 37

Horacio Saggion, Sanja Štajner, Stefan Bott, Simon Mille, Luz Rello, and Biljana Drndarević. Making it Simplext: Implementation and evaluation of a text simplification system for Spanish. *ACM Transactions on Accessible Computing (TACCESS)*, 6 (4): 14, 2015b. DOI: 10.1145/2738046. 60

Horacio Saggion, Stefan Bott, and Luz Rello. Simplifying words in context. Experiments with two lexical resources in Spanish. *Computer Speech and Language*, 35: 200–218, 2016. DOI: 10.1016/j.csl.2015.02.001. 22

Magnus Sahlgren. *The Word-Space Model: Using Distributional Analysis to Represent Syntagmatic and Paradigmatic Relations between Words in High-Dimensional Vector Spaces*. Ph.D. thesis, Stockholm University, 2006. 22

Helmut Schmid. Probabilistic part-of-speech tagging using decision trees. In *Proc. of the International Conference on New Methods in Language Processing*, Manchester, UK, 1994. 84

Alexander Schrijver. *Theory of Linear and Integer Programming*. John Wiley & Sons, Inc., New York, 1986. 55, 56

Sarah E. Schwarm and Mari Ostendorf. Reading level assessment using Support Vector Machines and statistical language models. In *Proc. of the 43rd Annual Meeting of the Association for Computational Linguistics*, ACL, pages 523–530, Stroudsburg, PA, 2005. Association for Computational Linguistics. DOI: 10.3115/1219840.1219905. 10, 12, 13

Violeta Seretan. Acquisition of syntactic simplification rules for French. In Nicoletta Calzolari (Conference Chair), Khalid Choukri, Thierry Declerck, Mehmet Ugur Dogan, Bente Maegaard, Joseph Mariani, Jan Odijk, and Stelios Piperidis, Eds., *Proc. of the 8th International Conference on Language Resources and Evaluation*, LREC, Istanbul, Turkey, May 2012. European Language Resources Association (ELRA). 1

Shai Shalev-Shwartz, Yoram Singer, and Nathan Srebro. Pegasos: Primal estimated sub-gradient solver for SVM. In *Proc. of the 24th International Conference on Machine Learning*, ICML'07, pages 807–814, New York, 2007. ACM. DOI: 10.1145/1273496.1273598. 19

Matthew Shardlow. A comparison of techniques to automatically identify complex words. In *Proc. of the ACL Student Research Workshop*, pages 103–109. The Association for Computational Linguistics, 2013. 24

Matthew Shardlow. Out in the open: Finding and categorising errors in the lexical simplification pipeline. In Nicoletta Calzolari, Khalid Choukri, Thierry Declerck, Hrafn Loftsson, Bente Maegaard, Joseph Mariani, Asuncion Moreno, Jan Odijk, and Stelios Piperidis, Eds., *Proc.*

of the 9th International Conference on Language Resources and Evaluation, LREC, Reykjavik, Iceland, May 2014. European Language Resources Association (ELRA). 22

Luo Si and Jamie Callan. A statistical model for scientific readability. In *Proc. of the 10th International Conference on Information and Knowledge Management*, CIKM, pages 574–576, New York, 2001. ACM. DOI: 10.1145/502692.502695. 10, 11

Advaith Siddharthan. An architecture for a text simplification system. In *Proc. of the Language Engineering Conference*, pages 64–71, 2002. DOI: 10.1109/lec.2002.1182292. 1, 35, 37

Advaith Siddharthan. Preserving discourse structure when simplifying text. In *Proc. of the European Natural Language Generation Workshop*, pages 103–110, 2003. 86

Advaith Siddharthan. Syntactic simplification and text cohesion. *Research on Language and Computation*, 4 (1): 77–109, 2006. ISSN 1570-7075. DOI: 10.1007/s11168-006-9011-1. 34, 75

Advaith Siddharthan. Text simplification using typed dependencies: A comparison of the robustness of different generation strategies. In *Proc. of the 13th European Workshop on Natural Language Generation*, ENLG, pages 2–11, Stroudsburg, PA, 2011. Association for Computational Linguistics. 36, 40

Advaith Siddharthan and Angrosh Mandya. Hybrid text simplification using synchronous dependency grammars with hand-written and automatically harvested rules. In *Proc. of the 14th Conference of the European Chapter of the Association for Computational Linguistics*, EACL, pages 722–731, Gothenburg, Sweden, April 2014. Association for Computational Linguistics. DOI: 10.3115/v1/e14-1076. 37, 90

Advaith Siddharthan, Ani Nenkova, and Kathleen McKeown. Syntactic simplification for improving content selection in multi-document summarization. In *Proc. of the 20th International Conference on Computational Linguistics*, COLING, Stroudsburg, PA, 2004. Association for Computational Linguistics. DOI: 10.3115/1220355.1220484. 74

Matthew Snover, Bonnie Dorr, Richard Schwartz, Linnea Micciulla, and John Makhoul. A study of translation edit rate with targeted human annotation. In *Proc. of the 7th Conference of the Association for Machine Translation in the Americas*, pages 223–231, August 2006. 91

Matthew Snover, Nitin Madnani, Bonnie Dorr, and Richard Schwartz. Fluency, adequacy, or HTER? Exploring different human judgments with a tunable MT metric. In *Proc. of the 4th Workshop on Statistical Machine Translation*, pages 259–268, Athens, Greece, 2009. DOI: 10.3115/1626431.1626480. 91

Seth Spaulding. A Spanish readability formula. *The Modern Language Journal*, 40: 433–441, 1956. DOI: 10.1111/j.1540-4781.1956.tb02145.x. 19, 67

Lucia Specia. Translating from complex to simplified sentences. In *Proc. of the 9th International Conference on Computational Processing of the Portuguese Language*, PROPOR, pages 30–39, Porto Alegre, RS, Brazil, April 27-30, 2010. DOI: 10.1007/978-3-642-12320-7_5. 47, 49, 69, 90

Lucia Specia, Sujay Kumar Jauhar, and Rada Mihalcea. SemEval 2012 task 1: English lexical simplification. In *Proc. of the 1st Joint Conference on Lexical and Computational Semantics*, SemEval, pages 347–355, Stroudsburg, PA, 2012. Association for Computational Linguistics. 27, 28

B. Srinivas. Performance evaluation of supertagging for partial parsing. In *Proc. of the 5th International Workshop on Parsing Technology*, Boston, 1997. DOI: 10.1007/978-94-015-9470-7_11. 34

Sanja Štajner, Maja Popovič, and Hanna Béchara. Quality estimation for text simplification. In *Proc. of the Workshop and Shared Task on Quality Assessment for Text Simplification (QATS)*, Portoroz, Slovenia, 2016. 92

Kai Sheng Tai, Richard Socher, and Christopher D. Manning. Improved semantic representations from tree-structured Long Short-term Memory Networks. In *Proc. of the 53rd Annual Meeting of the Association for Computational Linguistics and the 7th International Joint Conference on Natural Language Processing of the Asian Federation of Natural Language Processing*, ACL, pages 1556–1566, Beijing, China, July 26–31, 2015. DOI: 10.3115/v1/p15-1150. 92

S. Štajner, R. Evans, C. Orasan, and R. Mitkov. What can readability measures really tell us about text complexity? In *Proc. of the Workshop on Natural Language Processing for Improving Textual Accessibility*, NLP4ITA, Istanbul, Turkey, May 27, 2012. 15

Sownya Vajjala and Detmar Meurers. Readability assessment for text simplification: From analysing documents to identifying sentential simplifications. *ITL—International Journal of Applied Linguistics*, 165 (2): 194–222, 2014. DOI: 10.1075/itl.165.2.04vaj. 17

Vincent Vandeghinste and Ineke Schuurman. Linking pictographs to synsets: Sclera2Cornetto. *Proc. of the 9th Conference Language Resources and Evaluation* (LREC), 3404–3410. 70

Vincent Vandeghinste, Ineke Schuurman, Leen Sevens, and Frank Van Eynde. Translating text into pictographs. *Natural Language Engineering*, pages 1–28, 2015. DOI: 10.1017/s135132491500039x. 70

Sanja Štajner. Translating sentences from "original" to "simplified" Spanish. *Procesamiento del Lenguaje Natural*, 53: 61–68, 2014. 49, 63

Sanja Štajner and Horacio Saggion. Readability indices for automatic evaluation of text simplification systems: A feasibility study for Spanish. In *6th International Joint Conference on Natural Language Processing*, IJCNLP, pages 374–382, Nagoya, Japan, October 14–18, 2013a. 19, 90

Sanja Štajner and Horacio Saggion. Adapting text simplification decisions to different text genres and target users. *Procesamiento del Lenguaje Natural*, 51: 135–142, 2013b. 58

Sanja Štajner, Biljana Drndarević, and Horacio Saggion. Eliminación de frases y decisiones de división basadas en corpus para simplificación de textos en español. *Computación y Sistemas*, 17 (2), 2013. 62

Sanja Štajner, Richard Evans, and Iustin Dornescu. Assessing conformance of manually simplified corpora with user requirements: The case of autistic readers. In *Proc. of the Workshop on Automatic Text Simplification—Methods and Applications in the Multilingual Society*, pages 53–63, Dublin, Ireland, August 2014. Association for Computational Linguistics and Dublin City University. DOI: 10.3115/v1/w14-5606. 70

Sanja Štajner, Hannah Béchara, and Horacio Saggion. A deeper exploration of the standard PB-SMT approach to text simplification and its evaluation. In *Proc. of the 53rd Annual Meeting of the Association for Computational Linguistics and the 7th International Joint Conference on Natural Language Processing of the Asian Federation of Natural Language Processing*, ACL, pages 823–828, Beijing, China, July 26–31, 2015. DOI: 10.3115/v1/p15-2135. 84

Sanja Štajner, Maja Popovič, Horacio Saggion, Lucia Specia, and Mark Fishel. Shared task on quality assessment for text simplification. In *Proc. of the Workshop and Shared Task on Quality Assessment for Text Simplification (QATS)*, Portorož, Slovenia, 2016. 92

Tu Thanh Vu, Giang Binh Tran, and Son Bao Pham. Learning to simplify children stories with limited data. In *Intelligent Information and Database Systems*, LNAI, pages 31–41. Springer International Publishing, Switzerland, 2014. DOI: 10.1007/978-3-319-05476-6_4. 90

W3C. *Web Content Accessibility Guidelines (WCAG) 2.0*, 2008. http://www.w3.org/TR/WCAG20/ 63

Andrew Walker, Advaith Siddharthan, and Andrew Starkey. Investigation into human preference between common and unambiguous lexical substitutions. In *Proc. of the 13th European Workshop on Natural Language Generation*, ENLG, pages 176–180, Stroudsburg, PA, 2011. Association for Computational Linguistics. 31

Sandra Williams and Ehud Reiter. Generating readable texts for readers with low basic skills. In *Proc. of the 10th European Workshop on Natural Language Generation*, 2005. 73

Kristian Woodsend and Mirella Lapata. Learning to simplify sentences with quasi-synchronous grammar and integer programming. In *Proc. of the Conference on Empirical Methods in Natural Language Processing*, EMNLP'11, pages 409–420, Stroudsburg, PA, 2011. Association for Computational Linguistics. 9, 37, 49, 55, 57, 90

Krzysztof Wrobel. PLUJAGH at SemEval 2016 task 11: Simple system for complex word iden-tification. In *Proc. of the 10th International Workshop on Semantic Evaluation*, SEMEVAL, pages 953–957, San Diego, CA, June 16–17, 2016. DOI: 10.18653/v1/S16-1146. 25

Cathy H. Wu, Manabu Torii, K. Vijay-Shanker, Catalina O. Tudor, and Yifan Peng. iSimp: A sentence simplification system for biomedical text. In *Proc. of the IEEE International Conference on Bioinformatics and Biomedicine*, BIBM, pages 1–6, Washington, DC, 2012. IEEE Computer Society. DOI: 10.1109/BIBM.2012.6392671. 77

Qiang Wu, Christopher J. Burges, Krysta M. Svore, and Jianfeng Gao. Adapting boosting for information retrieval measures. *Information Retrieval*, 13 (3): 254–270, June 2010. ISSN 1386-4564. DOI: 10.1007/s10791-009-9112-1. 15

Sander Wubben, Antal van den Bosch, and Emiel Krahmer. Sentence simplification by mono-lingual machine translation. In *Proc. of the 50th Annual Meeting of the Association for Compu-tational Linguistics: Long Papers*, volume 1, ACL, pages 1015–1024, Stroudsburg, PA, 2012. Association for Computational Linguistics. 9, 25, 49, 57, 90

Wei Xu, Chris Callison-Burch, and Courtney Napoles. Problems in current text simplification research: New data can help. *Transactions of the Association for Computational Linguistics*, 3: 283–297, 2015. 84

Kenji Yamada and Kevin Knight. A syntax-based statistical translation model. In *Proc. of the 39th Annual Meeting of the Association for Computational Linguistics*, ACL, pages 523–530, Strouds-burg, PA, 2001. Association for Computational Linguistics. DOI: 10.3115/1073012.1073079. 52

Victoria Yaneva, Irina Temnikova, and Ruslan Mitkov. A corpus of text data and gaze fixations from autistic and non-autistic adults. In *Proc. of the 10th Language Resources and Evaluation Conference*, LREC, 2016a. 18

Victoria Yaneva, Irina Temnikova, and Ruslan Mitkov. Evaluating the readability of text simpli-fication output for readers with cognitive disabilities. In *Proc. of the 10th Language Resources and Evaluation Conference*, LREC, 2016b. 3, 18

Mark Yatskar, Bo Pang, Cristian Danescu-Niculescu-Mizil, and Lillian Lee. For the sake of simplicity: Unsupervised extraction of lexical simplifications from Wikipedia. In *Proc. of the 49th Annual Meeting of the Association for Computational Linguistics*, ACL, pages 365–368, 2010. 25

David Zajic, Bonnie Dorr, and Richard Schwartz. BBN/UMD at DUC-2004: Ropiary. In *Proc. of Document Understanding Conference*, 2004. 44

Qing Zeng-Treitler, Sergey Goryachev, Hyeoneui Kim, Alla Keselman, and Douglas Rosendale. Making texts in electronic health records comprehensible to consumers: A prototype translator. In *AMIA Annual Symposium Proceedings*, pages 846–850, 2007. 31

Ying Zhang, Stephan Vogel, and Alex Waibel. Interpreting BLEU/NIST scores: How much improvement do we need to have a better system? In *Proc. of the 4th International Conference on Language Resources and Evaluation*, LREC. European Language Resources Association, 2004. 48

Zhemin Zhu, Delphine Bernhard, and Iryna Gurevych. A monolingual tree-based translation model for sentence simplification. In *Proc. of the 23rd International Conference on Computational Linguistics*, COLING, pages 1353–1361, Beijing, China, August 2010. 9, 25, 49, 57, 83, 90

Author's Biography

HORACIO SAGGION

Horacio Saggion is an Associate Professor at the Department of Information and Communication Technologies, Universitat Pompeu Fabra (UPF), Barcelona. He is head of the Large Scale Text Understanding Systems Lab and a member of the Natural Language Processing research group (TALN) where he works on automatic text summarization, text simplification, information extraction, sentiment analysis, and related topics. His research is empirical, combining symbolic, pattern-based approaches, and statistical and machine learning techniques. Horacio is also an active teacher and student supervisor. He holds a Ph.D. in computer science from Université de Montréal, Canada. He obtained his B.Sc. in computer science from Universidad de Buenos Aires, Argentina, and his M.Sc. in computer science from UNICAMP, Brazil. Before joining Universitat Pompeu Fabra, Saggion worked at the University of Sheffield, UK, for almost ten years for a number national and European research projects developing competitive human language technology in the areas of text summarization and question answering. Saggion was also an invited senior researcher at the Center for Language and Speech Processing, John Hopkins University, USA, for a project on multilingual text summarization. He is currently a principal investigator in a number of national and European research projects in text summarization, text simplification, and information extraction.

Saggion has published over 100 works in leading scientific journals, conferences, and books in the field of human language technology. He has organized several international workshops in the areas of text summarization and information extraction and was also co-chair of the 2009 Symposium on Information and Human Language Technology (STIL) and chair of the 30th Conference of the Spanish Society for Natural Language Processing (SEPLN). He is co-editor of the book *Multi-source, Multilingual Information Extraction and Summarization*, Springer, 2013. He is a regular program committee member for international conferences such as ACL, EACL, COLING, EMNLP, IJCNLP, and IJCAI and is an active reviewer for international journals in computer science, information processing, and human language technology. Saggion has given courses, tutorials, and invited talks at a number of international events including COLING, LREC, ESSLLI, IJCNLP, NLDB, and RuSSIR. He has received a number of grants and fellowships throughout his research career from institutions including Fundación Antorchas, the Argentinian Ministry of Education, the Canadian Agency for International Development, and the Ramón y Cajal Research Program.